SMART MOVES MANAGEMENT

SMART
MOVES
MANAGEMENT

CULTIVATING WORLD-CLASS
PEOPLE AND PROFITS

JOHN THEDFORD

EMERALD
BOOK CO.

Published by Emerald Book Company
Austin, TX
www.emeraldbookcompany.com

Design and composition by Greenleaf Book Group LLC
Cover Design by Greenleaf Book Group LLC

Publisher's Cataloging-In-Publication Data
(Prepared by The Donohue Group, Inc.)

Thedford, John.
    Smart moves management : cultivating world-class people and profits / John Thedford. -- 1st ed.
    p. : ill. ; cm.
    Includes bibliographical references.
    ISBN: 978-1-934572-29-0
1. Personnel management. 2. Corporate culture. 3. Success in business. 4. Pawnbroking--United States--Management. I. Title.

HF5549 .T45 2009
658.3   2009930900

Part of the Tree Neutral™ program, which offsets the number of trees consumed in the production and printing of this book by taking proactive steps, such as planting trees in direct proportion to the number of trees used: www.treeneutral.com

Printed in the United States of America on acid-free paper

09 10 11 12   10 9 8 7 6 5 4 3 2 1

First Edition

Dedication

SMART Moves Management *is dedicated to the investors, customers, and past and present team members—in thanks for the mutual support, commitment, and belief that when a business values all people, the results will follow. You're the living proof.*

CONTENTS

Author's Note: Why I Wrote *SMART Moves Management*   xi

Pawnshop IQ Test   xiii

Introduction: Our Strategic Path   1

CHAPTER 1
Results: *How Do You Do That?*   9

CHAPTER 2
Prosperous Wage Strategy: *Your Starting Hourly Pay Is* What?   17

SMART Move 1:	Use the Prosperous Wage Strategy to your advantage.	21
SMART Move 2:	Expect healthy turnover, but fight unhealthy turnover.	23
SMART Move 3:	Set no maximum wages for any position.	27
SMART Move 4:	Pay the individual, not the team, for performance.	29
SMART Move 5:	Measure individual productivity.	31
SMART Move 6:	Have a simple compensation plan.	34
SMART Move 7:	High wages to decrease costs.	35
SMART Move 8:	Use weekly pay as a great motivator.	37
SMART Move 9:	Remember that we are professionals.	38
SMART Move 10:	Practice "overstaffing"; it's never as expensive as understaffing.	40
SMART Move 11:	Apply the experience curve to performance.	42

CHAPTER 3

Identification of Strengths: *How Do You Hire?* 47

SMART Move 12: Win with strengths. 52

SMART Move 13: Hire the hungry, not the starving. 54

SMART Move 14: Adopt a rigorous selection process. 55

CHAPTER 4

Right Fit: *How Do You Place the Right Person in the Right Role?* 59

SMART Move 15: Assess performance along a hard line: stay or go. 63

SMART Move 16: Implement broadbanding in answer to the Peter Principle. 65

SMART Move 17: Root out the "brotherhood of the miserable." 68

SMART Move 18: Recruit full-time employees only. 70

SMART Move 19: Conduct regular reviews of every employee. 72

SMART Move 20: Believe that there are no unimportant jobs. 73

SMART Move 21: Promote an egalitarian versus an elitist approach. 74

SMART Move 22: Expect excellence in every role. 77

CHAPTER 5

Right Training: *How Do You Train Your Team Members?* 81

SMART Move 23: Send employees to a company learning center. 84

SMART Move 24: Build business intelligence with book reviews. 86

CHAPTER 6

Great Managers: *How Do You Build Such Consistency of Performance Throughout the Company?* 91

SMART Move 25: Create limits on span of control. 105

SMART Move 26: Discover the benefits of long-term training programs. 105

SMART Move 27: Create a lease line. 106

SMART Move 28: Play chess instead of checkers. 107

SMART Move 29: Build bench strength. 108

SMART Move 30: Calculate the cost of turnover. 109

CHAPTER 7

Great Teams: *How Do You Build Your Teams?* 115

SMART Move 31: Calculate your return on hiring. 129
SMART Move 32: Live the Golden Rule. 131
SMART Move 33: Be wary of roast beef issues. 132

CHAPTER 8

Engaged Employees: *How Do You Keep Your Employees so Satisfied and Productive?* 137

SMART Move 34: Give employees an informal Q^{12} survey. 145
SMART Move 35: Once you know what's broken, fix it! 146
SMART Move 36: Develop a path toward leadership behavior. 147

CHAPTER 9

Engaged Customers: *How Do You Acquire Such Loyal, Profitable Customers?* 149

SMART Move 37: Build the business for the Right Customer. 156
SMART Move 38: Do not outsource customer service. 157

CHAPTER 10

Sustainable Growth: *At What Point Do Your Stores' Revenues Peak?* 161

SMART Move 39: Do not move people around. 166

CHAPTER 11

Real Profit Increase: *Aren't All Profits Real?* 169

SMART Move 40: Know what you mean by profit. 175
SMART Move 41: Make profits possible. 176

CHAPTER 12

Stock Price Increase: *How Do You Measure the Health of
the Company?*   179

CHAPTER 13

"The Very Point of Life": *Why Do You Care so Much About Your
Team Members?*   185

CHAPTER 14

Final Words: *How Does Being "All About People" Lead to Consistent
Performance and Profitability?*   197

BIBLIOGRAPHY   203

ABOUT THE AUTHOR   205

AUTHOR'S NOTE:
WHY I WROTE
SMART MOVES MANAGEMENT

The thoughts and ideas for this book came during the long and enjoyable process of operating Value Financial Services, one of the most successful businesses of its kind. I am an entrepreneur, and I do not think or write in the same way as many who deal heavily in theory and premise. I think and act squarely in terms of what is actionable and profitable for the business.

I have spent a great deal of time also looking at the best practices of many other operations. This book brings together the particular actions that, in my opinion, will make any business successful. To that end, I had four audiences in mind when I sat down to put my thoughts on paper. They are as follows:

- **General Business Audience:** These include the businesses out there that really want to be the best they can be—and don't mind changing to make things better.
- **Prospective Team Members:** What better way to attract talent than to have a guidebook to business success that developed according to our company's values and standards?

- **Current Team Members:** This book also serves as a guide for our team members, to clarify, codify, and maintain the culture and business philosophy that has been a proven part of our company's success.

- **Business Associates:** I wanted our business associates, vendors, bankers, and anyone else who might do business with us to know who we are and how we have become successful.

I know there are many how to books out there, but I see little that is actionable in those books. It is a waste of time to talk about issues but take no action. At our company, our culture helps us stay on course when talking about change, so we can act upon anything that could help us become a better business operation.

Well-known and successful CEOs like Jim Sinegal (Costco) are quoted frequently in the media regarding what makes a business successful. Their central theme is simple and easy to understand: The rank-and-file employees must maintain the culture, business philosophy, and corporate discipline that enables them to do the right thing over and over without becoming disengaged. To achieve this goal, these business leaders add, you must hire for excellence in every role. I do this in my business dealings

I hope you enjoy reading my book. It is an easy read with actionable information throughout. Enjoy your way to greater profitability!

—*John Thedford*

PAWNSHOP IQ TEST

Before we get started, I invite you to review the Pawnshop IQ Test that follows. It reveals the misperceptions that most people outside our industry have about pawnshops. You may be surprised.

- **What is the average size loan at pawnshops?**
  The average loan is $115.
- **What percentage of loans are redeemed (paid off)?**
  More than 80 percent of all loans are redeemed.
- **What percentage of the U.S. adult population has no banking relationship?**
  Forty percent of the U.S. adult population has no relationship with a banking institution.
- **What is the size of the pawn industry in the United States?**
  The pawn business is an $8 billion industry.
- **What percentage of transactions in the industry deal with stolen property?**
  Less than one-tenth of 1 percent of pawn transactions deal with stolen property.

OUR STRATEGIC PATH

PEOPLE ARE THE CORE OF OUR STRENGTH. Not just anybody, but the right people. Our Strategic Path provides well-defined criteria and standards that help us identify, develop, and retain the right people. Think of it as the backbone or structural spine supporting the body of our business. Along our Strategic Path are ribs or refinements, called SMART Moves, that fill it out even further. Our corporate culture puts flesh on the bones and breathes life into the business, so we can serve our customers and reward our investors.

We've learned a great deal from Gallup Consulting, both as clients and from its published works. With permission, we've modified The Gallup Path—from Appendix A of the book *First, Break All the Rules*, by Marcus Buckingham and Curt Coffman—for our use. (This and a

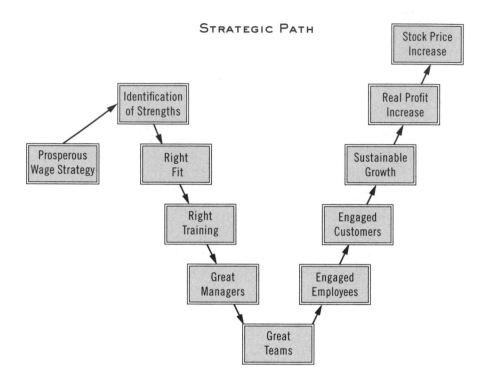

STRATEGIC PATH

host of other great references are listed in the Bibliography at the end of this book.) Gallup sought to answer the question, what is the path to sustained increase in shareholder value? Starting with the investor in mind, the company provided key stations along a prescribed route to profit. The opening paragraph from the book's description of The Gallup Path reads

> Through research examining the linkages between key elements of a healthy business, the Gallup Organization has developed a model that describes the path between the individual contribution of every employee and the ultimate outcome of any business: an increase in overall company value.

Indirectly, the authors are referencing the SMART Moves Triangle of interconnected elements: employees, customers, and investors.

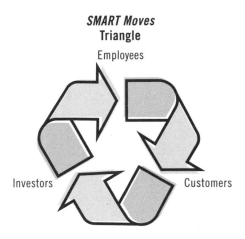

**SMART Moves
Triangle**

Employees

Investors

Customers

NOT A MODEL, BUT AN EQUATION

How many times have you been asked to explain your business model? At its core, this statement is wrong: Business success is not a model. It is an equation of compatibility and chemistry among Engaged Employees, customers, and investors. We look at our Strategic Path and the SMART Moves Triangle as much more than just a business model. We see a very successful and meaningful equation that will produce Engaged Employees, who in turn will provide exceptional customer service and make so much money for themselves and for the company that our shareholders will marvel at the outcome. We consider this a kind of chemistry that develops between our team members and our customers. For us, the simple equation that tells us two plus two equals four is the same as following our Strategic Path to increased earnings for everyone, including our loyal shareholders, who believe in this equation as much as we do.

This introduction begins with a brief overview of our Strategic Path; the chapters that follow detail each waypoint along its length—each box shown on the previous page. Most chapters present several SMART Moves—tidbits and details to further illuminate your understanding of our approach. Think of our Strategic Path as being like the rules of golf that apply to any golfer on any course. SMART Moves, on the other hand, are akin to the local ground rules unique to a particular course. They bring depth to each milestone along our Strategic Path.

Note that SMART Moves also are cross-referenced throughout the book, using a shorthand notation within a set of parenthesizes. For example, "(SMART Move 13)" would indicate a reference to "SMART Move 13: Hire the hungry, not the starving." The cross-references are a convenient reminder and locator of key concepts.

With the help and guidance of our SMART Moves, our management team is charged with designing, maintaining, and improving our Strategic Path. Business life before we developed our Strategic Path was good, but life *with* the Strategic Path is *great*! Joe Genovese, a team member, says, "When you follow our Strategic Path, failure is never an option."

Our Strategic Path is a path lined with gold—and not for our company alone. It is especially valuable for distributed workforces, such as retailing, branch banking, car rental companies, and other scattered working groups. Each step on our Strategic Path is part of a planned and conscious decision invested with thought, mistakes, money, and man-hours as it was conceived, designed, developed, and built. We're relentlessly learning and improving along the length and breadth of our Strategic Path, thanks to our relationship with Gallup Consulting and our tenacious desire to *get better every day*.

According to Henry Ford, men must be led into prosperity. Our Strategic Path is our means for making that happen. It is a highly developed and carefully designed method that blends people and processes into world-class performance at each point on the SMART Moves Triangle. Marking the length of our Strategic Path is a progression of key milestones. Each waypoint leads to the next to form linkages between key elements of a healthy business.

The entrance to our Strategic Path is a *Prosperous Wage Strategy*. Within our industry, we pay the highest wages and offer the greatest earning upside potential—it's part of our mission. Very few retailers compare to the compensation and benefits package we make available to our team members. This enables us to attract a larger candidate pool of talented people to the company. Our sales associates can give themselves a raise as often as they like, because their earning potential is unlimited.

Next, in every candidate and team member we seek to achieve the *Identification of Strengths*. We use a tool to develop a strong concept of who will succeed in various positions in the company, based on individuals' strengths. A candidate can be placed where there is a *Right Fit* of person and position. Once we have hired the right person with the right strengths to the right role, we invest heavily in the *Right Training* for each team member. This involves working with *Great Managers* who further team members along in their career and professional development.

Great Managers are constantly training team members on the day-to-day aspects of our business, familiarizing them with every step along our Strategic Path. Our training is not just on-the-job mechanics. We're training entrepreneurial people as sales associates who are more naturally inclined to think, act, and make rapid decisions within the structure and culture of the team. At this point, they just need training and experience in our way of doing business, which focuses on personal productivity and team play. As a result, our teammates are constantly innovating and sharing best practices. As King Solomon says in Eugene H. Peterson's *Living the Message*, "You use steel to sharpen steel, as one friend sharpens another."

The investment in these first five steps gets us to the base of the check mark: *Great Teams*. Our goal is excellence in every role and a great team in every store and headquarters department. Every effort preceding the Great Teams node on the Strategic Path is an investment made in personal productivity and team formation. From this point, our return on investment is both sustainable and predictable. A Great Manager with a Great Team assimilates, trains, and develops employees to become *Engaged Employees*—each a team member who is the right person in the right role with the right incentives, behaviors, and rewards. Engaged Employees on a Great Team backed by a Great Manager naturally perform at high levels. Positive rewards, a sense of competence, visible achievement, and clear recognition translate into high employee retention and reduced costs of doing business across every line item on the income statement. In this manner, our Prosperous Wage Strategy is further rewarded.

Engaged Employees have proven to be profitable for us because they attract *Engaged Customers*. These enthusiastic fans of our company become repeat customers, an active army of word-of-mouth crusaders who recruit their family and friends to our stores. Our positive customer relationships create *Sustainable Growth* in terms of new and existing customer transactions and the accompanying financial performance. A loyal and active customer base thus fuels *Real Profit Increase*—not through acquisitions and accounting manipulation, but because our cost of doing business decreases while the frequency of customer transactions increases. This type of indigenous growth means that the core value of the company rises, creating a *Stock Price Increase* for our shareholders. In turn, we can further enhance our Prosperous Wage Strategy, which allows us to cycle another round of improvements to every aspect of our Strategic Path.

MORE THAN A CHECK MARK

In addition to the eleven milestones portrayed in the figure that represents our Strategic Path, there is another, more subtle lesson. Every milestone on the left side of the check mark is an investment leading us to Great Teams. Every milestone on the right side of the check mark creates a return on that investment. Our Strategic Path requires an investment in selecting and equipping team members to expect and achieve extraordinary success, especially compared to their peers outside of our company.

Our Strategic Path is not a theoretical model for us. It is our way of doing business every moment of every day. When you understand our Strategic Path and how it informs our corporate culture, you will gain insight on why and how we score so strongly in national measures of employee and customer engagement. Work with us and learn who we are, how we envision success, and what we do to achieve it—and your life and career will be transformed.

INTRODUCTION SUMMARY

KEY POINTS

- Our Strategic Path is our plan to be the best, and it is shared with every team member. This creates clarity about our definition of success and how we get there.
- Our Strategic Path focuses our efforts in a systematic manner to identify, develop, and value contributing members of our team.
- Our Strategic Path is a visual representation of the integration of our values, method of valuing people, and creating wealth.

CHAPTER I

RESULTS:
HOW DO YOU DO THAT?

The performance of your stores is exceptional, and your employee turnover is as low as I have seen. Now, just explain to me how you did that."

Tom Morris, Orlando, Florida, retired Sears marketing executive

"REALLY? How do you do that?"

This is the most frequently asked question by people outside our company once they discover our perennial world-class results in profits, employee engagement, and customer engagement. The short answer — we value people. The longer answer is found within the pages of this book. Our consistent results are hard won by being true to our Strategic Path and to a daily series of reinforcing and aligning disciplines called SMART Moves. In other words, our expected results are by design, not by chance.

To many in the business world, the only thing that really matters is the results. Results are telling, it's true—but they give an incomplete picture. Open the *Wall Street Journal* and you can read the opening and closing prices for stocks; this tells you what happened to the stock price that day, but it says nothing about the company and its people. Your local sports section carries the box scores of the baseball game, but the incredible, game-winning double play is not in the experience. Results inform, but they don't tell the story.

In *SMART Moves Management*, you're getting behind the box scores, beyond the headlines and highlights. You're going deep into the story. Our business is now designed and documented with a core ideology and approach that informs our business systems and corporate culture, to create a world-class customer experience and a high return for investors.

THE SMART MOVES TRIANGLE

The three most important groups of people in the life of our company are our employees, our customers, and our investors—in that order! The interplay of these groups tells the real story of our company. Results for shareholders are forged through a business platform that rewards employee productivity, team play, and profitability. This is pursued in the context of serving customers who return to shop and refer their family and friends. In the presence of the right corporate culture, the unwavering pursuit of profit demands the best from everyone on the team so we can all win—but not at the expense of each other.

On the next page is the SMART Moves Triangle that represents the dynamic interdependence of these three audiences. For an organization to reach its fullest potential, each corner of the Triangle must be thriving. Throughout *SMART Moves Management*, this pattern repeatedly emerges.

You may remember the hand game called Rock, Paper, Scissors. The object of the game is simply to determine a winner and a loser. You may recall that it goes like this: rock breaks scissors; scissors cut paper;

and paper covers rock. In many companies, the game is played competitively among employees, customers, and investors, with each attempting to gain the upper hand. Pitting groups against each other may give a temporary advantage to one group, but it results in an unhealthy business climate and performance where everyone loses, though they may think they're winning.

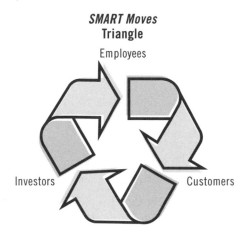

SMART Moves
Triangle
Employees

Investors   Customers

In contrast to the Rock, Paper, Scissors game is our employees-customers-investors relationship. Here is a true means of creating wins for all stakeholders. It requires each player to have a deep understanding and appreciation of the other groups' unique contributions, a profound sense of give-and-take, and the desire to build and participate in something greater than him- or herself. Greed is the enemy of this system, while mutual profit making is the grease that keeps every part moving. As soon as one party "goes for the kill" and succeeds, the power of the SMART Moves Triangle to create wins for everyone breaks down.

The Triangle may seem to be a delicate balancing act to maintain. In fact, once developed, it is a highly stable and extraordinarily productive system of corporate leading and development.

In plain English, here's what the Triangle says: Happy employees are more likely to produce happy customers, who give us more of their dollars and then tell more of their friends about us. This, in turn, increases revenues, reduces costs, increases profits, and makes our investors happy. The investors reward the employees with better pay, benefits, and opportunities. This obviously makes the employees even happier, and so the Triangle cycles upward. The most striking thing about this system is the stewardship each group must hold for the others. Self-interest must be tempered by following the Golden Rule of Life: "Do unto to others as you would have others do unto you" (SMART Move 32).

THREE STAKEHOLDER MEASURES

When we focus first on people, the rest of the business becomes an exercise in managing details. This includes three elements: employee engagement, customer engagement, and profit per store. The measure of each element provides the most reflective snapshots of our past and future performance, helping us to ensure sustainable profitability and increase shareholder value.

For each measure, a third party audits our results so we can be certain that we're not fooling ourselves. Our external financial auditor—RSM McGladrey, Inc., a leading business accounting and tax firm—ascertains profit per store. To gauge employee and customer engagement, we hired Gallup Consulting, a division of Gallup, Inc.—most famous for the Gallup Poll. This unique consultancy within the Gallup family of companies specializes in employee and customer management to inform leaders on how to improve business performance. Gallup has served us well since 2003, helping us refine and accelerate what we were already inclined to do. (No sense reinventing the wheel—especially as it's a thoroughly validated wheel.)

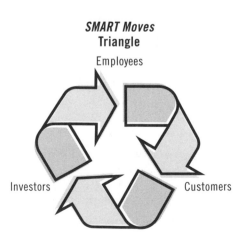

SMART Moves Triangle

Employees

Investors

Customers

The vital importance of the SMART Moves Triangle to our business was intuitive and the triangle was refined by hard trials and lessons. In 2002, I read the book *First, Break All the Rules*, by Marcus Buckingham and Curt Coffman of Gallup Consulting. I found that their research, thinking, and methods confirmed our observations, experience, and efforts. The benefit of referring to outside experts is that they have studied a situation repeatedly while we may have faced it once or twice. While we may see only the problems, consultants see the larger picture and the *cause* of the problems. This "big picture" perspective helped me get a handle on the three most important reflections of our sustainable results: employee engagement, customer engagement, and profit per store.

1. *Employee engagement* is an internal gauge of the team members' sense of significance, accomplishment, belonging, and competence on the job. Highly engaged employees tend to engage customers through an improved customer experience, and this links directly to profitability.

2. *Customer engagement* is a long-term measure indicating loyalty, advocacy, and brand experience. A high level of customer engagement points to external wellness and goodwill, and also links directly to profitability.

3. *Profit per store* reflects the proper integration of equipping employees and treating customers right while still being true to the shareholders who took the risks to create the company and who stand strong with our approach. Profit per store is also an ideal indicator of operational productivity and effectiveness.

This may all sound simple in theory, but the question, how do you do that? emerges again, this time focused on our corporate culture.

When Gallup reports to us, it benchmarks our employee and customer engagement numbers against its vast database of more than 8 million respondents. Both metrics are reduced to a percentile compared with Gallup's responses across industries and countries, from seven decades of work with more than ten thousand clients. Participating companies include The Ritz-Carlton Hotel Company, The Walt Disney Company, Starbucks Corporation, Best Buy, and Chick-fil-A, to name but a few. We take pride in the fact that our accomplishments are in the same category as these world-class brands.

Now, let's take a look at how we measure up when we get our reports on employee engagement, customer engagement, and profits per store.

- **Employee Engagement:** We're in Gallup's "Best Practice" category for employee engagement. This means we are in the top 16 percent of all clients surveyed, a status we've achieved every year since 2003—the year we began working with Gallup Consulting. We score at the 84th percentile—just below the "World Class" category, which begins at the 90th percentile. We're steadily improving, however, and we feel confident that we'll break into Gallup's World Class category in a few years.

- **Customer Engagement:** We are rated by Gallup as "World Class" (in the top 10 percent) in customer engagement, with a 92nd percentile ranking. Gallup's outside assessment validates what we are doing and helps us improve it even more. Our customers are dedicated fans, and we're dedicated to further improving our standing among the world's best.

- **Profits per Store:** Our company has been the world's most profitable chain of pawn stores on a per-store basis and in terms of return on investment—period. No publicly traded competitor comes close. We're not just leading the industry—on profit per store, we're lengths ahead. In other words, our employees perform where it matters most: face-to-face with the customers in the store. Not to be outdone, our headquarters team contributes systems and expertise to help the field team members be effective and efficient in our retail locations. Our shareholders are well rewarded for their investment.

I'm proud of these results and I tout them regardless of whether I'm talking to prospective employees, potential investors, other CEOs and businesspeople, Wall Street analysts and commentators, or media interviewers.

A BILLION-DOLLAR BLUEPRINT

For a high-growth, high-potential business like ours, *SMART Moves Management* is the blueprint to a future multibillion-dollar-a-year business. That's the vision.

SMART Moves Management codifies and illuminates a significant portion of our business model and company culture as they're integrated along what we call our Strategic Path—a highly defined, documented, and measured pathway to citizenship within our company. We're rigorous in our selection and performance expectations, starting with our employees but also including customers and investors. A great deal of this book is dedicated to describing this transformational means of repeatedly leading ordinary men and women to become extraordinary performers.

Our Strategic Path is a fundamental investment in the sustainable growth and profitability of this company and its people. This succinct understanding of what makes us successful provides an enduring yet flexible core to our future. If you're a reader who is hungry for an entrepreneurial opportunity in a fast-paced, competitive, and rewarding environment that encourages true service and respect, then you are welcomed here.

Let's talk money. First, we pay a prosperous wage and offer a rich benefits package. Are you motivated to work harder so that you will earn more money? Thanks to our performance-based compensation plan, some of our retail sales associates earn a substantial living. Many store managers take home six figures. Compare that to other retailers where a frontline "clerk" may be making just above minimum wage. Our sales associates start at more than double the minimum wage and are immediately trained to increase their earnings through service to our customers. As the saying goes, we're looking for a few good men and women.

Those readers outside our company will come to understand that what we have is a world-class business model as robust, dynamic, scalable, and responsive as most any business you will come across. My hope is that other businesspeople will be inspired to think more profoundly and intentionally about their charge, be it the receptionist desk, a sales territory, a store, a cash drawer, or the presidency of the company.

Used car dealers and pawnshops are often held in similar "esteem." CarMax redefined the used car business category; we've been redefining the pawnshop category for well over a decade. We're good neighbors and corporate citizens wherever we locate a store. It is the right way to live . . . and it happens to be good for business. The best way I can describe our standing in this business is to tell you that we are the Ritz-Carlton of the pawn industry. Remember, we focus on our team members and our customers, and this drives our profits year after year.

This is a simple overview of our results. You're invited to get beyond the box scores, however—to learn about the people and manners of our company. The SMART Moves Triangle is reflective, not prescriptive; that is, it is a representation of who we aim to serve, not a strict portrayal of any particular role that must be followed. Please don't miss this essential point: *SMART Moves Management* is about our human resource strategy and is based on a heartfelt belief in the inherent value and worth of people. So if you've been asking, how do you do that? then keep reading and you'll learn exactly how.

CHAPTER SUMMARY

KEY POINTS

- Financial results alone reflect past performance. Future financial performance, however, is more easily predicted based on customer and employee measures.
- The SMART Moves Triangle is represented by employees, customers, and investors. The metrics we use to determine our success are employee engagement, customer engagement, and profit per store.

CHAPTER 2

PROSPEROUS WAGE STRATEGY: *YOUR STARTING HOURLY PAY IS* WHAT?

Cutting wages does not reduce costs—it increases them. The only way to get a low-cost product is to pay a high price for a high grade of human service and to see to it through management that you get that service.

Henry Ford, *Today and Tomorrow*

ACCORDING TO OUR MISSION STATEMENT, WE WILL HAVE THE "HIGH-EST PAID AND WEALTHIEST TEAM MEMBERS IN THE INDUSTRY." And we do. In this case, the results speak the truth, loud and clear. We don't just say this in our mission statement; we actually plan for, measure, and act upon it. These aren't just words on paper to us. We live them.

The Prosperous Wage Strategy really is a strategy more than a program, compensation plan, or initiative. This leading marker on our Strategic Path invigorates the entire check mark. The goal is for our people to receive an abundant wage with an upside potential that is based

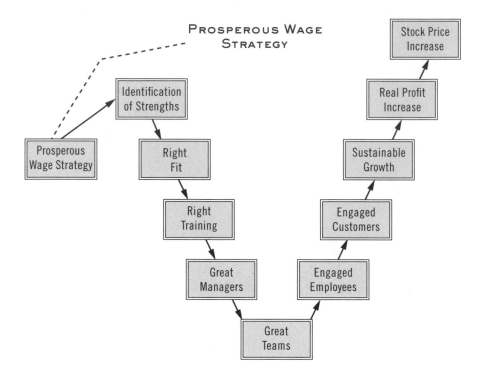

on personal performance, plus the security of a substantial enterprise within an entrepreneurial environment.

Earnings are personal, and we understand that. We know that well-paid employees who become engaged in their work over time develop expertise that accrues to the company's performance and profits. Therefore, pay-for-performance must be expressed in clear terms that are publicly understood and easily calculated.

Embedded in the minds of most businesspeople is the notion to reward success with pay increases. We, too, believe in rewards. (Not to boast, but being selected to be on our team is a reward in and of itself!) Pay raises for our sales associates, however, are self-determined through their performance. We hire the hungry, not the starving (SMART Move 13); our team members are hungry to earn and produce, and through their work they create their own schedule of raises.

Unlike other companies, however, we actually *start* with a high wage base. The foundation of our Prosperous Wage Strategy is our base hourly pay rate. The U.S. minimum wage of $6.55/hour set on July 24, 2008, reveals that the term *living wage* is a politician's misnomer for "barely getting by financially." Both the minimum wage and the living wage are flawed and meaningless concepts that actually hold wages down instead of raising them. By comparison, our starting hourly rate for new sales associates is $12 to $15 per hour, plus upside performance-based bonuses that typically amounted to an additional $2 to $3 per hour. We have sales associates with earned bonuses earning more than $60,000 per year.

At our company, you are one of a team of about ten people in a neighborhood store serving a surrounding customer base that you often know on a first-name basis. Not only do you get paid well, you're respected and liked because you are able to help people. Yes, transactions are where we make our money. The relationships formed around the transactions, however, are how we've built our business.

We want our team members to earn as much money as possible. Their mastery of their profession begets company success. Mastery makes money and saves money in every aspect of the business. Training returns dividends for the life of the team member.

Long-tenured team members are extraordinarily well trained, talented, and suited for the job. Headhunters from other retailers frequently recruit our people. A national retail chain recently pushed for one of our top sales associates to join it as a store manager. The company wooed her with a title, benefits, and an upward-trending career path. "You don't have to work in a pawnshop" was its big closing line.

The inevitable topic of compensation arose. She revealed what she was earning and was met with incredulity. Her pay stubs verified her claim. The store manager job offer would have translated into a significant pay cut from her current earnings as an hourly associate. To match her present compensation, she would have needed at least two promotions to become a regional manager, a position that required extensive traveling. Meanwhile, with our company, she earns a great living; works a normal workweek; sleeps in her own bed every night; is recognized for her competence, confidence, and accomplishment; earns perks; and enjoys a far superior benefits program.

Our wage strategy paid off defensively in this case. Her loss would have resulted in unwanted employee turnover, which could have cost us hundreds of thousands of dollars in profits over several years—not to mention the priceless inspiration, leadership, and training she provides to sales associates throughout the company.

Some might argue the fact that pay is typically a less important factor motivating employees. This reflects a lack of understanding of how people affect every line on the company's income statement. Why not provide interesting work, a sense of accomplishment, *and* a prosperous wage with upside earning potential? Basic stuff, really. Yet almost every candidate we interview for employment is underpaid by our standards. High turnover is the most common complaint in the retail industry, as well as the most expensive issue facing that business. A low wage strategy is the root of the problem.

The Prosperous Wage Strategy also provides an offensive position from which to attract remarkably talented people to our company. That is, it allows us to be extraordinarily selective when hiring.

Our stores are not filled with high-priced "warm bodies" that can't get the job done. On the contrary, we staff our stores with team members we have assessed as being capable of embracing our way of doing business. In advance, each team member is deemed worthy and capable of performing far beyond the potential of the average person. The first reward for new hires is the simple act of being offered a position. From there, you have access to a lifetime of opportunities.

SMART MOVE 1

Use the Prosperous Wage Strategy to your advantage.

Put the right person in the right role, and pay people what they're worth based on their performance.

"Where did you get the idea for your Prosperous Wage Strategy?" is another frequently asked question. This approach emerged in a moment of near death for the business, thanks to the pain of nearly going bankrupt a decade ago. It was a "school of hard knocks" lesson that was affirmed by the books I was reading at the time. Perhaps the lesson would not be so inextricably embedded in our strategy if I didn't have the scars to show for this difficult season, and if I hadn't found those affirmations and insights in my reading materials.

It was 1998, and with forty existing stores we were charging along and growing. An infusion of equity allowed us to quickly open forty new stores and thus double in size. This growth was far too quick. The debt and equity structure was wrong, and the interest on loans burdened the business. Finances got out of whack, and our banker called our line of credit. Covering payroll was a week-to-week war as we fought off the bank to find $350,000 from anyone—investors, family, friends, suppliers—to cover payroll. We were in full-on survivalist mode for nearly three years.

We had eighty stores, and nobody was helping. In fact, people were bailing out left and right. The investors fled for the hills. The bankers hit the bunkers and shot out demands. Even highly placed officers in the company said we were done.

Everyone's advice was to cut payroll. Yet this kind of panic has never made sense to me. We simply needed to get back to the fundamentals of our business. We had region leaders and stores, lots of stores, that weren't performing. Many of the region leaders had been promoted from store managers and either were at the wrong level or were being paid as region leaders but weren't fully trained into it. Two of my best former managers were now region leaders, but I needed them each to run a store again.

Weighing the options, I discovered that a need for fast results meant a realignment of talent. Those two region leaders would be more valuable running a store—even at their current high wage—because without a doubt, they would produce earnings. Similarly, some top-notch sales associates were working as store managers but were struggling. Similarly, these people could do the sales and lending job because they had proven track records of performance. Well-paid, capable people working within their strengths made good business sense.

I had discovered how to put my stores in great hands.

Why not pay each person their current wage but place them back where they could win—and win *big*—for themselves and the company? Reposition the people, but keep their pay high and give them incentives to make even more money. This proved to be the ticket out of the financial squeeze. In short, the strategy was simple: Put the right person in the right role and pay them what they're worth plus a portion of what they contribute. Respect the position, and let your people shine as superstars.

Our vice president of operations thought the repositioning plan was ridiculous. He said, "None of these people will take a cut in title and roles." In fact, he wanted to fire the people who were stretched in their present roles but had been proven winners in previous positions. He didn't buy into any of these ideas, because he had little appreciation for the plight of his people. Each individual was struggling, wasn't having fun, and might actually embrace the opportunity to return to known strengths. So instead of taking the VP's advice, I fired him for not valuing the people and went ahead and moved everyone to where they had been proven winners. It worked!

That's when I realized that together, high wages for the right role and having the right person in a high-performance job doesn't create problems—it works your way out of them. People solve problems and take advantage of opportunities; engaging their brains pays off. Placing highly paid and talented people on the front lines running our stores proved so successful, I sought to expand the Prosperous Wage Strategy throughout the company.

I read *The Loyalty Effect* back in 1999 when I was going through all this mess. It kept referencing Henry Ford's books, so I started reading them next. In essence, Ford faced similar struggles in the early twentieth century with the Henry Ford Company. Ford said, "I'm going to double wages and get the best people we can find to come work every job, from the janitor to the engineer to the top-level executive." He raised average daily wages from two dollars to five dollars and watched profits take off. I thought, *That's the recipe*, so I applied it with vigor.

Though Ford created an industrial empire, later generations dismantled it as they moved away from his methods and genius. Interestingly, Toyota copied Henry Ford in detail, and today it is number one in the automotive world by almost any positive measure.

Truth be told, this deep wound to the business in the late 1990s brought about our Prosperous Wage Strategy. In retrospect, it is easy to see why it's the only way to go: It is doing right by people rather than taking advantage of them. Why not gather the best people you possibly can and allow them to invest their brains and talents—in fact, their lives—in the growth of the business? High wages work!

SMART MOVE 2

Expect healthy turnover—fight unhealthy turnover.

Healthy turnover is when a team member who doesn't fit our values and performance standards is removed from the company. *Unhealthy turnover* is when a productive, Right Fit team member resigns for reasons within our control; this is extraordinarily detrimental to profits.

People leave managers, not companies. So much money has been thrown at the challenge of keeping good people—in the form of better pay, better perks and better training—when you have a turnover problem, look first to your managers.
Marcus Buckingham and Curt Coffman, *First, Break All the Rules*

In the case of *healthy turnover*, the person simply needed to pursue a new future in order to use his or her talent and strengths in a fresh venue. This is a good thing for both parties. An excessive amount of healthy turnover, however, may indicate a possible breakdown somewhere in the selection process—a potential systemic problem. This would mean the company has an even bigger problem than the impact of just one employee.

Unhealthy turnover, on the other hand, must be avoided. The cost of unhealthy turnover directly affects profitability and indirectly affects *every* item on the income statement. There is no reason why unhealthy turnover should occur within our stores.

Some turnover is inevitable. We will lose great team members because of life situations outside our or even the employee's control. In these cases, we can only grieve the loss of a colleague and wish the person well in his or her new endeavors.

Our leadership team's monthly review of turnover helps us catch trends in both healthy and unhealthy turnover. We work to get beneath the numbers to the real story of what is happening. This assessment provides us with an early warning system about sustainable real profits. If a manager is having turnover problems with sales associates, then that manager's hiring practices and procedures may need a refresher, a reminder, or perhaps supplemental assistance from the training department in order to remedy this negative pattern.

There is a direct correlation between store manager continuity and profitability. Turnover is, therefore, one of our leading indicators of profitability. In other words, continuity of competent managers is the single most important contributor to sustaining profits. Frederick F. Reichheld says in *The Loyalty Effect*

> In most of the industries we've studied, the companies with the highest retention rates also earn the best profits. Relative retention explains profits better than market share, scale, cost position or any of the other variables usually associated with competitive advantage. It also explains why traditional management techniques often backfire in chaotic ways.

A sizable investment in managers is made because the return on investment is unlimited. Before being assigned as a store manager, manager candidates enter a lengthy training program that can last from twelve to twenty-four months. During this time, they are learning the business from the perspective of both a sales associate and an assistant manager prior to learning the role of a store manager. There are no shortcuts to qualification when the standards and measures are demanding. Results prove the point.

Our investment in managers, however, pays like an annuity over the life of the manager's career with us. We are the most profitable organization in our industry on a per-store basis. Our average net income per store in 2008 was just shy of $480,000. Of our publicly traded competitors, the closest was about $225,000 and the lowest competitor was $150,000. We outperformed our closest competitor by 55 percent and our most distant by 130 percent.

As the Store Manager Continuity Chart on the next page shows, our store managers who run a store for less than one year averaged $375,000 in store-level net income. Simply put, our newest managers outperformed our closest competitor's average store net income. We attract winners! And that's just the beginning. Our managers' performance keeps improving as the magic of mastery kicks in, and the net income begins a dramatic climb as continuity increases. Our store man-

STORE MANAGER CONTINUITY CHART

Net income per store over the last 12 months (vertical axis, 150,000 to 850,000)

Manager tenure in the same store (horizontal axis: Less than 1 year, 1–2 years, 2–3 years, 3–6 years, 6+ years)

agers who have been in the same store three-plus years outperform our closest competitor's stores by 194 percent!

There are no company-imposed limits to a store's growth. For example, in 2008, one of our Atlanta stores, managed by a seven-year team member, produced more than $1 million in net income. Nipping Atlanta's heels was a ten-year manager in West Palm Beach and a nine-year manager in Orlando, with store net income of more than $900,000 each.

Continuity pays big-time. The Manager Continuity Chart tells the dramatic story of keeping people in the same store. Let's clarify what we mean by continuity—*the same manager at the same location over time.* Continuity is different than tenure. Tenure is length of employment with the company; continuity is length of service in the same store. In the rare instances when we do move a manager, it is for a really sound reason. Managers tend to sink roots in their neighborhood store much like any small business owner would do. Their customers can count on them being in the same store day after day. Continuity is a fancy way of saying that relationships, trust, history, and experience matter immensely in the human psyche—and for profitability. It also speaks to the fact that you cannot move people around without experiencing a loss!

I find it perplexing that so many retailers and companies feel compelled to use what they call "management rotation." This so-called best practice rotates store managers under the guise of keeping them fresh, broadening their experiences, and cross-training them. If you want to keep them fresh, then don't give them boring work! Provide them with the opportunity to cultivate depth of experience and a sense of ownership. Give them the freedom to build relationships, serve customers, and surround themselves with a great team. Don't uproot them and then wonder why they lack consistency and commitment! Sinking roots speaks to our people.

Losing good people is a killer to any organization. Unhealthy turnover is the enemy of our business and a cancer to our Strategic Path. The loss of productive team members for reasons within our control is tragic. We hire people for a lifetime and make a significant up-front investment in their training and development. Turnover cuts short the return on that investment.

SMART MOVE 3
Set no maximum wages for any position.
Place no limits on the earning potential of any human being. This practice benefits neither the person nor the company.

There can be no "standard" wage. No one on earth knows enough to fix a standard wage. The very idea of a standard wage presupposes that invention and management have reached their limit.

Henry Ford, *Today and Tomorrow*

We place no limits on the earning potential of our team members. As a person adds value to our customers and, in turn, to our company, that person must be allowed to participate in the value created. Our unlimited upside earning potential means that performance is *always* rewarded. We make it worthwhile for the top performers to stay on board with us.

We want the best and the brightest Right Fit people for our business. Ceilings on pay and bonuses will inevitably drive the best and brightest out of any company to pursue their own gains. Why discourage entrepreneurial people by withholding rewards for excellence? It makes no sense, yet I hear of it all the time, especially in sales organizations.

Rewards, however, must be tempered with discipline. Every great athlete knows that discipline creates freedom, innovation, and unmatched performance. The reason a gymnast can "stick a landing" is because of the discipline involved leading up to this next level of performance. We coach team members to a higher level of mastery and, like athletes, they are apt to surprise us all by doing what was thought to be impossible. Their creativity and innovation play off of our own. Limits are just that—impediments to productivity, real success, and greater earnings. Removing limits on earnings will open the path to unparalleled performance.

Innovation is an everyday event at our company, and frankly, it is a joy to watch. Only those who are intensely thinking about improving their pay, performance, and customer service can do what our people accomplish. Corporate headquarters can dictate "best practices" to the field, but in reality, we can only make space for our employees to share learning, ideas, and lessons born out of actual wins and losses. We're a highly social company because we know the best innovations are often shared over a team dinner celebration or when just spending time together.

Experience tells me that management rarely devises frontline innovations. Management's main innovation is to find better ways to foster an environment conducive to risk taking and value creation. Then we pollinate the best ideas and examples across the company and acknowledge remarkable performance. Management doesn't inspire; great performance does.

SMART MOVE 4
Pay the individual, not the team, for performance.

Despite the noblest of intentions toward individual performers, team-based financial incentives inevitably reward slackers and punish producers.

This is an important aspect of our Prosperous Wage Strategy. For our sales associates, we have no team-based financial incentives; all incentives are based instead on individual performance. A team incentive for individual performers risks confusing and discouraging personal excellence. Team measures are unfair to our sales associates 100 percent of the time! (Managers, however, are rewarded based on store net income each month, which is considered indicative of their individual performance.) Despite the noblest of intentions, this system far too often rewards the loafers and punishes the go-getters. The business pays the price, and that means the employees pay the price. Don't mess with personal productivity and pay.

This lesson dates back to the early 1620s and the Pilgrims. After landing at Plymouth Rock, they lived in a commonwealth setting whereby everyone "benefited" from what the community produced. Distribution was based on need. It was an unmitigated disaster leading to widespread starvation—not because of harsh winters, but because of harsh human realities. Governor William Bradford wrote in *Of Plymouth Plantation* about his experiences in those early years, stating that the commonwealth system "was found to breed much confusion and discontent and retard much employment that would have been to their benefit and comfort." He goes on to say, "Young men, that were most able and fit for labour, did repine that they should spend their time and strength to work for other men's wives and children without any recompense." In other words, poor personal incentives produced little food and raised animosity within the Colony.

To remedy the matter, Bradford reports, the Colony devised a new means of production using private property assigned to each family for personal cultivation. What you grew, you kept, traded, or sold. The results speak for themselves. Bradford says the change "had very good success, for it made all hands very industrious, so as much more corn was planted than otherwise would have been." Personal incentives modified behaviors: "The women now went willingly into the field and took their little ones with them to set corn; which before would allege weakness and inability." By dropping the communal approach, the Pilgrims never again faced starvation. They thrived socially, economically, and spiritually. Hence, a new nation was born.

Even Bradford's theology was amended, thanks to the private property approach. In a *National Review Online* article, James S. Robbins reports, "Bradford believed the new arrangement was a much more accurate reflection of the will of God. He who had made men different, who gave them varying abilities that they might employ them in the manner He intended." Bradford's writings are remarkable insights into the social workings of humans pitted against extreme hardship. When we need each other the most, we tend to act in our immediate self-interest even to the detriment of our long-term self-preservation.

Given today's socioeconomic and political landscape of entitlements, one can only wonder if the Pilgrims' colonial lesson has been lost. They talked with their neighbors about what methods worked and didn't work to produce the harvest. Sharing ideas with each other is what decent, caring people do. Just imagine a group of these Pilgrims sitting around discussing the good and bad of the recent harvest. This is how Bradford saw the new colony, and this is what worked for them.

This system of balanced competition and cooperation works for our sales associates, too. Every sales associate has a cash drawer from which he or she conducts and grows business. Sure, our people like to compete against each other, but only in the way of spurring themselves on to even bigger victories. Competition tends to bring out the best in people, yet each team member knowingly depends on others to service their customers, maintain the store, and create a welcoming environment. They need one another in order to provide a culture of winning.

Managers are like William Bradford in that they supervise the overall effectiveness of a store. They are paid based on the performance of the team, and they must keep the team functioning. They are charged with holding together individuals who work in the same store but out of a private drawer.

Instead of having group financial incentives, a compensation plan that mimics a failed communal system of production, we embrace the importance of personal productivity on the front lines of our stores.

SMART MOVE 5
Measure individual productivity.

Our "economic denominator" is what we call *productivity*. Every person in store operations and line management has a written personal productivity goal that is measured weekly.

We did notice one particularly provocative form of economic insight that every good-to-great company attained, the notion of an "economic denominator." Think about it in terms of the following question: If you could pick one and only one ratio—profit per x—to systematically increase over time, what x would have the greatest and most sustainable impact on your economic engine?

Jim Collins, *Good to Great*

Productivity begins with our sales associates, the frontline customer contact people; each has an individual productivity goal. Sales associates are managed by an assistant manager or manager who is paid on the cumulative results of the store. A region leader is paid on the cumulative results of his or her reporting stores. The director of operations oversees all region leaders and is paid on the cumulative results of all stores. In turn, the board of directors looks to me, as CEO, to make sure that store operations and headquarters staff are producing a solid return on investment. Suffice it to say, my incentives are tied to the overall performance of the company.

For the sales associate, failure to meet the stated productivity goal initiates a series of preprogrammed events that can ultimately result in being fired for failing to meet one's goal. It is a highly objective system but not a ruthless one. It flags problems fast, so we're getting to the source of them within days instead of weeks or months. Problems don't have much time to go unaddressed because there is a clear demonstration of how they have hurt business. New hires are often stunned to learn that productivity goal tracking happens in near real time. Our sales associates are informed about this concrete standard and know that the box score benefits everyone. It is designed to be a win-win situation, and everyone loves to *win*!

This numbers approach may seem out of place and even cold in a corporate culture that prides itself on kindness. Let's not confuse coldness with accountability, however. First, these ground rules for measurement are stated right up front in the hiring process. Second, these are highly objective minimums set at realistically obtainable levels. Because of the strength of our Strategic Path, we know what to expect. We are all on the same team. This system depends on everyone pulling their weight. If a person consistently fails to perform, then we have to cut the person or else our entire system loses integrity. If someone isn't getting the job done for which they were hired, then it is unfair to ask other high-performing team members to protect an underperformer. Finally, if someone isn't being successful with us, it only makes sense that the person move to a new opportunity where he or she may be better suited for success. This tough-love mind-set works.

Let's put some numbers to this and let you see how our learning, training, and productivity combine to elevate our results. Below are the actual productivity goals for our sales associates over the last five years.

SALES ASSOCIATE WEEKLY PRODUCTIVITY GOALS

2003	$5,000
2004	$6,000
2005	$7,000
2006	$8,000
2007	$11,000
2008	$12,000

What jumps out is the growth in the goal over the years. One might mistakenly assume this is the old-school method of "management by objectives." On the contrary, these goals reflect across-the-board business improvement mostly as a result of having Right Fit people. These goals also apply across the board to both our newest and our longest-tenured sales associates. As every aspect of our business model improves and our company culture solidifies, we're attracting people who are better suited to our team and more likely to succeed. Our training keeps improving and better preparing them to excel and get up to speed quickly. Our newest sales associates are typically beyond the minimum productivity goals within four to five weeks.

Setting the bar in writing is the right thing to do; this way, associates always know where they stand. Only when it is written does it become "real."

Let's look at the details. Here is the 2008 productivity goal of $12,000 "over and under" standard: Fall below $9,000 six out of thirteen weeks and you get a letter saying you need to improve. If you are below $9,000 eight out of thirteen weeks you're fired or repositioned to a more suitable role. On the other hand, rise above $15,000 and you earn bonuses. Every year the productivity goal is adjusted based on our expectations. As a result, we get better every day!

We are in the business of helping people succeed and dramatically exceed the minimums. In 2008, our top-producing sales associates produced from $18,000 to $25,000 weekly in productivity. Think about it—one person generating $900,000 to $1,250,000 per year from his or her drawer of business (and that's with two weeks or more of vacation thrown in!). Seen in this light, it is an amazing statistic.

In our system of productivity goals we have a method that provides rapid feedback, excellent training, and high reward, and that sets a reasonable bar to sustain employment. Measuring individual performance every week works.

SMART MOVE 6

Have a simple compensation plan.

Our company's simple compensation plan means that every team member can readily figure out how to make money for the company and how that impacts his or her weekly commission check. An immediate sense of where one stands against personal performance goals at any moment in time is a powerful posture and incentive for each person.

Complex compensation plans leave people guessing until calculations are completed and posted—typically monthly or quarterly. Those affected can become suspicious that some programmed "black box" is being manipulated to cheat them of their due. Complex systems of compensation are a lot like filing one's tax returns with the IRS. Try as one might to be honest and forthright, there's always this small voice in the back of one's brain, saying, *I hope this is right.*

Ultimately, our business involves a high-volume, low-ticket, detailed transaction between a lender and a borrower. Government regulations, extensive paperwork, serial number checks, and fingerprinting must be done right. There's a high cost per transaction, which has to be off-set with comparable charges. Nevertheless, team members need to be quick-minded with customers. Computers don't tell us values; they simply help us compute. The end decision rests with a live person, so we work to keep the compensation plan simple.

At the end of a day's, week's, or month's worth of transactions, all associates know to the penny where they stand. For our team members, few things are as empowering as the feeling of being on top of your drawer and earnings at any given moment. Associates can go home at night not only knowing the box score for that day, but also well aware of what needs to happen the next day. This self-managed approach works, especially with our more entrepreneurial team members.

Results for all store team members are posted weekly. In our competitive culture, you better believe personal performance is compared against one's peers.

SMART MOVE 7
Wages are not a one-to-one expense. High wages decrease costs.

Cutting payroll to produce profits is a one-time trick with long-term negative consequences. Paying a prosperous wage and expecting more from your people will increase productivity and produce more profits.

Buying labor is just like buying anything else—you have to make sure you get your money's worth.

Henry Ford, *Today and Tomorrow*

Henry Ford had it right. When management pays a prosperous wage to the people who take care of the customer, the shareholder wins. If management takes profits out of the pockets of the people who take care of the customer, then the sustainability of the business is dramatically diminished. Team members (or "labor," as Ford put it) are the essential component for making a business work. Cutting payroll to produce profits may provide limited short-term benefits but it has long-term negative consequences.

Most businesspeople I come across today, however, would say that Ford's thinking is counterintuitive; this is because they manage line items on the income statement instead of considering the *whole* of the business. Lost are the macroeconomic and sociological perspectives on the interconnection of people, performance, and profits. The absence in most organizations of something along the lines of our Strategic Path means the potential of the SMART Moves Triangle becomes a missed opportunity. This relationship isn't managed or measured, so mediocrity gains a foothold.

Our company, on the other hand, provides a unique opportunity for a prosperous wage plus upside earning. We're in the business of leading people to prosperity. Discounting wages only discounts profitability.

We're not alone in our approach. One of my hero companies is Costco. The average wage earned by its team members is $18/hour. That is about three times the national minimum wage. If you are a Costco shopper for any length of time at the same location, you'll notice the same people working in the same store for years. Costco understands continuity in stores, and its practices encourage tenure with the company. The company saves a bundle in turnover costs while also increasing customer engagement and loyalty. Does loyalty pay? Absolutely! Costco's monthly sales as reported in the *Wall Street Journal* prove that it is a consistent financial winner in the retail sector.

Because our service is positively proactive, keeping our employees happy is good for business. Our sales associates earn upside reward by caring for customers, and our customers develop a trust that keeps them coming back for more. We require our associates to take down names and contact information for transactions. In turn, they get to know the customers, their families, and their needs. Our team members are like personal shoppers, in a manner of speaking. Our inventory is always changing, and customers can't keep up with what is in the stores. If your sales associate knows that you want an Apple iPod and one becomes available, then you will be called and invited to come in and buy it or put it on layaway. If you have pawned an item and you are about to forfeit it for lack of payment, then you'll get a courtesy call reminding you to redeem it. It's amazing how many people forget about redeeming their pawns; without our call, they would forfeit something they really wanted to keep.

Low wages imply a cheap return, while high wages set a high expectation. High wages encourage a much greater level of productivity, which benefits all involved.

SMART MOVE 8
Use weekly pay as a great motivator.

Compensation is an important part of any employment arrangement. Aside from a clear understanding of how we pay our team members, our company also takes the necessary steps to make sure everyone is paid correctly and on time.

Paying correctly, on time, and for the shortest time frame possible is the genius of a successful business. There is no substitute for this kind of policy in any company.

Our past experience tells us that paying on a weekly basis is by far the best way to go. Weekly pay allows all our employees to understand how they are paid, the time frame for which they are being paid, and how bonuses or commissions are paid. Each team member can predict how much he or she will be paid any given week simply by looking at individual productivity and base rate of pay. This provides a great motivating tool for everyone.

Paying less often than every week can leave things open to confusion and misunderstanding. It can also create feelings of doubt in the minds of those who are waiting on bonus or commission payments. The system of personal productivity commissions can lose much of its motivational value to team members if payment is made only once or twice per month. There is simply no good reason not to operate this way.

It is our position that we should always pay for the shortest time frame possible—weekly—to allow every team member to focus on what they can earn next instead of wondering how much they will be paid two or three weeks out. Plainly put, it works.

SMART MOVE 9
Remember that we are professionals.
Our culture of learning is comprehensive, and training never ends. When people discover *why* and *how* their work makes a difference and meaningfully connect the two, they gain a significant winning advantage.

You expect a civil engineer to have a solid understanding of Newton's Laws of Motion and a firm grasp of certain principles of physics and math. You expect a doctor to have a profound understanding of organic chemistry and anatomy. You expect a business lawyer to grasp constitutional law and the Uniform Commercial Code. In short, you know that these professionals have a systematic, deeper understanding of the principles upon which their profession is established and according to which it functions.

On the other hand, you probably don't expect a retail salesperson or manager to be versed in practical principles and practices of business, sales leadership, and management. Each of our team members is a professional businessperson. They are not retail clerks hemmed into a mindless existence as merely a cog in the corporate wheel. Many of our retail counterparts view people as a necessary line-item expense on the income statement when in fact people are the very essence of what makes the income statement produce on the bottom line.

In 2008, our stores averaged almost $2 million each in total revenue. Each store acts as a small business, with each store manager earning an income comparable to that of a small-business owner—perhaps a five- or six-figure income on these revenues. Yet our store managers don't carry the full entrepreneurial risk and workload, and they have the support of our entire operation.

In the world of business, most people have on-the-job training specific to the task at hand, but often they haven't been exposed to the underlying principles. They understand their duties and responsibilities, but not necessarily the principles that helped create them. Like the old adage, it is like giving someone fish so he can eat for a day instead of teaching him how to fish so he can feed himself for a lifetime.

Hiring any "warm body" at the lowest price kills retail service and will eventually kill the business. I know of retail establishments that hire someone as an assistant manager one week and promote him or her to a store manager role the next. How can someone know the culture and methods of a business in less than two weeks? Slack hiring standards reflect a cavalier attitude toward people. This elitist mind-set is destructive at any level of the organization.

We are raising up a legion of prosperous professionals and business-people. Success depends upon being versed generally in business and economics, and in particular on the specifics of our industry. Informed businesspeople are more apt to make better business decisions and thereby improve their contribution and value to the company. Rewards are sure to follow. In turn, greater contribution means lower costs, better customer service, and higher earnings across the store and the company. That means we can attract even better people by perpetuating our Prosperous Wage.

SMART MOVE 10

Practice "overstaffing"; it's never as expensive as understaffing.

We hire the right people when we find them, not just when we need them. So-called overstaffing creates productive time for thinking, planning, and serving the customer.

Keeping more people than you need on staff can generate greater profits if management sees to it that associates' time is used wisely. This management strategy actually proves to be cheaper than understaffing, because the customer is "touched" more often and cared for more thoroughly. This is one of the most difficult SMART Moves to grasp for the average businessperson who is taught to manage personnel costs tightly. Waste is not being advocated here. Capacity to serve and improve every day is the real agenda.

Putting extra people on the schedule doesn't mean they'll be idle when customers aren't in the store. Numerous productive alternatives are available to our associates and managers, all aimed at improving operations and working conditions. Downtime for team members is invested wisely in calling customers, planning a promotion, arranging a display, cleaning the store interior, picking up parking lot litter, training, and so forth.

Overstaffing as a strategy also means that we hire Right Fit people when we meet them, not just when we need them. Our rigorous selection process takes time to interview, assess, hire, and train the right people. Maintaining a large staff that is ready for expansion or unplanned turnover is a practice designed to increase profits. If we're hiring only when we have openings, then we're behind in the game and constantly playing catch-up.

Overstaffing is certainly a difficult move for store managers charged with meeting net income goals, because an "extra" hire creates the impression that expenses will be higher but won't translate into higher profits. But improved customer service, employee continuity, and less stress *do* contribute to greater profits. While other managers can waste chunks of time fine-tuning staff schedules to match customer traffic patterns, ours don't; we default to overstaffing, which frees the manager to be with team members and customers rather than micromanaging the roster.

Marriott Hotel management has a concept it calls "marble time." The reception area is overstaffed to give managers and front-desk people time to stand on the customer side of the counter—"where the marble is"—and provide random acts of customer service or point out employees who are available to help. Getting out from behind the counter also gives the manager a different perspective on what's happening in the hotel as guests come and go.

According to one Harvard Business School professor writing in the *Harvard Business Review* (March 2008), "My research shows that increased staffing levels are associated with better execution behind the scenes in places like the back room, and that stores with better execution have higher profits." This may be because overstaffing provides a comfortable margin that works in the favor of the customer. Engaged customers talk and tell their friends. Overstaffing works!

SMART MOVE 11
Apply the experience curve to performance.

Whether it is throwing a baseball, performing heart surgery, or filling out a loan application, the more one does an activity, the faster, better, and more efficient one becomes. Practice does make perfect! That's the "experience curve" at work.

The "learning curve" is an economics principle generally applied to the production of hard goods. When the concept is applied to people who are learning new skills, such as delivering a service like pawn brokering, it is called the "experience curve." The more experience someone has with doing a job, the more proficient that person becomes. He or she is inclined to make fewer mistakes and to find ways of improving productivity. This has the effect of lowering the overall cost of services, meaning an increase in overall profitability. Therefore, experienced employees generally entail the lowest labor cost—which makes employee retention the key to profits. It follows that highly experienced and productive employees are the most profitable. This is why our company has developed its practice of profit sharing through commissions and bonuses, which invites employees to seek productivity gains through innovation.

A sales associate will be productive within weeks of completing our initial orientation program. Over the next several months, he or she will continue to learn about different kinds of merchandise, build customer relationships, and grow more comfortable with creating multiple transactions. Mastery of the position—versus just getting the mechanics right—requires experience, and we understand that it just takes time to get fully up to speed.

We've learned that it takes about twenty-four months in a training role before a new store manager becomes fully competent. Refer once more to the Store Manager Continuity Chart (page 38) as a reminder of the financial horsepower of the experience curve. Keeping managers in the same store is a dramatic predictor of store net income and reward for store managers. Because we are armed with this information, we can inform managers who are new to a store what they can expect along the road ahead. In fact, this knowledge gives us all a sense of comfort and supports the notion that patience is rewarded. When a store manager fails to hit typical numbers for the store, we issue an early warning that corrective measures may be needed to help the manager get back on track. This banding together of peers by tenure and continuity has proven to be invaluable; our insight relative to performance attracts, develops, retains, and inspires our managers. The manager who trusts the process and works hard can anticipate significant financial rewards and recognition.

Our company employs an experience curve when we hire, train, and promote team members, especially as it relates to measuring the development of our management ranks. We look at each member of our store and headquarters teams and compare their performance to that of their banded peers. This assessment allows us to consider the performance of a manager in a role for only three months in a different light than one who has been in management for several years.

In some instances, it is necessary to rank every management team member based on performance against every other person in that role across the organization. However, banding peers provides a high degree of perspective for management at all levels, as opposed to pressuring every manager regardless of continuity. It is a humane and right reflection of expectations.

When we experience unhealthy turnover (i.e., the loss of a highly experienced manager), it costs us dearly because the effect of that person's experience curve is lost to us. The loss comes not only when store operating net income potential is cut short, but also in terms of training—that person's ability to impart experience to newer associates and future managers.

CHAPTER SUMMARY

KEY POINTS

- The Prosperous Wage Strategy defies conventional business wisdom but makes good business sense when one understands how turnover affects every line on the income statement.

- The Prosperous Wage Strategy tends to attract a larger and more qualified candidate pool, meaning selection can be more rigorous.

- The long-term objective of the Prosperous Wage Strategy is retention of highly trained and experienced employees who build customer goodwill, lower overall operating costs, grow profits, and continuously improve shareholder value.

SMART MOVE 1

Use the Prosperous Wage Strategy to your advantage.

Thanks to the pain of nearly going bankrupt a decade ago, I learned to put the right person in the right role and to pay people what they're worth based on their performance.

SMART MOVE 2

Expect healthy turnover—fight unhealthy turnover.

Healthy turnover is when a team member who doesn't fit our values and performance standards is removed from the company. *Unhealthy turnover* is when a productive, Right Fit team member resigns for reasons within our control; this is extraordinarily detrimental to profits.

SMART MOVE 3

Set no maximum wages for any position.

Place no limits on the earning potential of any human being. This practice benefits neither the person nor the company.

SMART MOVE 4
Pay the individual, not the team, for performance.

Despite the noblest of intentions for individual performers, team-based financial incentives inevitably reward slackers and punish producers.

SMART MOVE 5
Measure individual productivity.

Our "economic denominator" is what we call *productivity*. Every person in store operations and line management has a written personal productivity goal that is measured weekly.

SMART MOVE 6
Have a simple compensation plan.

Our company's simple compensation plan means that every team member can readily figure out how to make money for the company and how that impacts his or her commission check. An immediate sense of where one stands against personal performance goals at any moment in time is a powerful posture and incentive for each person.

SMART MOVE 7
Wages are not a one-to-one expense. High wages decrease costs.

Cutting payroll to produce profits is a one-time trick with long-term negative consequences. Paying a prosperous wage and expecting more from your people will increase productivity and produce more profits.

SMART MOVE 8
Use weekly pay as a great motivator.

Compensation is an important part of any employment arrangement. Aside from a clear understanding of how we pay our team members, our company also takes the necessary steps to make sure everyone is paid correctly and on time.

SMART MOVE 9

Remember that we are professionals.

Our culture of learning is comprehensive, and training never ends. When people discover *why* and *how* their work makes a difference and meaningfully connect the two, they gain a significant winning advantage.

SMART MOVE 10

Practice "overstaffing"; it's never as expensive as understaffing.

We hire the right people when we find them, not just when we need them. So-called overstaffing creates productive time for thinking, planning, and serving the customer.

SMART MOVE 11

Apply the experience curve to performance.

Whether it is throwing a baseball, performing heart surgery, or filling out a loan application, the more one does an activity, the faster, better, and more efficient one becomes. Practice *does* make perfect! That's the "experience curve" at work.

CHAPTER 3

IDENTIFICATION OF STRENGTHS: *HOW DO YOU HIRE?*

First, you must identify the employee's individual strengths. In step two, you must position that individual to perform a role that capitalizes on these strengths. Failure to meet these two requirements cannot be corrected by either the employee's motivation or expert coaching.

Marcus Buckingham and Curt Coffman, *First, Break All the Rules*

PRESIDENT ABRAHAM LINCOLN HAD A WAR TO WIN, BUT HE NEEDED A GENERAL TO FIGHT IT FOR HIM. Lincoln didn't fancy himself a military man, but as president he was pressed into the role of commander in chief during the Civil War. So he sought counsel from the experts, beginning with seventy-five-year-old General Winfield Scott.

Lincoln discovered that preparing for war and fighting a war are mightily different. He learned that most generals were preparers, not fighters; reactive, not proactive; and containers, not chargers. He

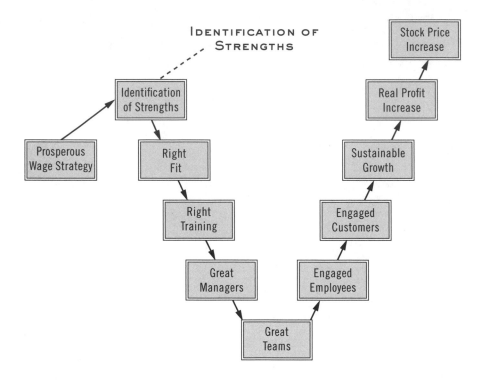

concluded that trial and error and on-the-job training was an expensive way for a president to wage a war and pick generals.

Over a period of two bloody years, Lincoln went through a "parade of generals" as described by Donald T. Phillips in *Lincoln on Leadership.* What Lincoln's generals told him about waging war and how they performed in the field didn't square with the president. But one general stood out from the rest in terms of performance: Ulysses S. Grant. Lincoln's war experts derided Grant as a drunk who lacked military finesse, intelligence, and an acceptable public persona. Regarding Grant's drinking, legend is that Lincoln quipped, "Because of the many lives we are losing and the significance of this great battle, if I knew the flavor of General Grant's favorite beverage I would send it to the other generals." In fact, Grant was not a drunk as he was often portrayed to be, but a humble and reluctant man who was thrust into a role and performed his duty with genius.

What Lincoln knew about Grant was this: *Grant won battles*. Over the advice of his "experts," Lincoln appointed Grant lieutenant general of the Army of the United States, a rarely used title in the history of the country. Grant's brilliance proved successful in both winning the Civil War for the North and mending relationships with the South. In fact, his character and gracious manner eventually landed him in the White House as president.

HIRING FOR STRENGTH

The point of the Lincoln and Grant story is that genius doesn't always come in a nice, neat package that fits comfortably on the shelf of the human resources department. Author and management expert Peter Drucker says, "Where there are tall peaks, there are deep valleys." Our company is egalitarian, not elitist, in our hiring (SMART Move 21). People who have endured hardships often have the fortitude needed to succeed in life. Just because one may not be a "safe hire" by typical standards, it doesn't mean one can't be talented in the workplace.

Weaknesses cannot be fixed; they can only be managed. Great racehorses are often high-strung and might even throw riders. The jockey must minimize the danger while encouraging the thoroughbred to do what it does best: race. Selecting people for their strengths and learning to work with their weaknesses is a day-to-day challenge, but a stable full of racehorses will beat plow horses any day.

Traditionally, people are hired based on experience, education, and background—which makes for safe and predictable choices. The past, however, is often not the best predictor of talent. We look for innate abilities that *underpin* a person's experience, education, and background. How a person "looks" on paper and how he or she plays on the field can be decidedly different. We have studied the team members who've turned out to be our best, regardless of education and experience, and that is who we are after: more of the *best*!

Digging deeper in the hiring process means we invest less time playing the "fix-'em-up game" with people who don't belong; there's no sense in putting round pegs in square holes. Once we focused on hiring strengths and talent, our people decisions became clearer and simpler. Our candidate qualifications narrowed, and that made identification easier even though it required a larger, more exhaustive search area.

Photos of our top sales associates and managers hang on my office wall to remind me that some of our absolute best talent didn't have a lick of experience in sales or retail before we hired them—but it turned out they could close sales, care for customers, and excel in our business. It is so easy to get knotted up on experience and education that we forget that all we really need is talent in the areas we've identified as important.

If Lincoln had had to fight another war, he would've benefited from his two-year learning curve in hiring and replacing generals. Here's where we've learned our lessons about hiring talent; we're well into our learning curve. Being well past the trial-and-error stage *and* having learned what talent works within our business model, we are rigorous in selecting people who are Right Fits.

It is a huge recruiting and hiring advantage when you know what to look for in your "Grants." The experts tell us that personalities don't really change much from the time we're about eleven years of age—that's called our "temperament." We don't debate that statement; we embrace it. Hiring the right temperament into the operations side of our business is both a science and an art that we take seriously. The rest of our Strategic Path relies on getting great talent into our system.

David Johns, our vice president of administration, worked at Sears, Roebuck and Co. when that company was in its prime. Today, we use a predictive tool that he used at Sears: the Thurstone Temperament Schedule. This questionnaire was first used in a business setting in the early 1950s. It assumes that well-adjusted people need to understand their dominant, stable traits as being different from and similar to other functional persons. Like any such assessment, it has its limitations and so is meant to supplement our judgment, not replace it. We have tested the very best of our employees in every position, and remarkably, they all score within the same range. Thus we are able to use the assessment to focus on hiring more of our proven performers.

We hire individuals who have high *performance* dimensions for being active, impulsive, dominant, emotional, and social; at the same time, we look for a much lower *reflective* dimension. These performance dimensions, as indicated by the Thurstone Temperament Schedule, are our gateway predictors of talent. This tool works for us, having proved to be a powerful ally in our quest to identify persons with the right mix for our defined needs.

UNNATURAL STRENGTH

Gallup Consulting is a prominent proponent of the strength movement. In short, Gallup says that Great Managers *focus on* people's strengths and *manage around* their weaknesses. It seems like common sense, but it is not common practice in the business community or even in life. A child brings home a report card with five As and a B, and Dad asks what went wrong with the B. A professional golfer bemoans what went wrong in today's round of 70 at Augusta National—it should have been a 66.

Why do we overly focus on what we *can't* do instead of what we *can* do? We naturally gravitate toward problems. The strength movement is founded on inviting people to move away from their natural tendency of dwelling on their weaknesses and to begin building on their strengths instead.

We can learn. Our strengths are where our true talents and abilities reside; they allow us to make a difference. We're more apt to succeed in our areas of strength than away from them, in areas of weakness. Repairing weaknesses is exhausting work. By constantly focusing on our flaws, we fall short on exploring our strengths. Our approach, therefore, is to play to people's strengths!

We ask, train, and equip people to move away from their natural tendency of focusing on weaknesses—theirs and others'. Of course, those with significant weaknesses are sent on their way to find an opportunity better suited to their strengths. But for those suited to our business, we look at their strengths in getting the job done and offer a measure of grace regarding their weaknesses.

When you attend a performance, you are paying to be entertained. The personality of the performer is irrelevant as long as his or her behavior doesn't spill over negatively into the act. You are entertained by the performer's excellence, and this justifies the price of the ticket.

We identify the strengths we need in specific roles across the company, and we are fully invested in this process. The Thurstone Temperament Schedule helps us identify the strengths we need in our positions by assessing our top performers for similar attributes. We then match these profiles to people whose strengths align with the position. Is there any other way to win?

SMART MOVE 12
Win with strengths.

In Jack Welch's book *Winning*, which is read and discussed throughout our organization, he presents his 4-E (and 1-P) framework for evaluating talented people. We apply it to our talent identification system in order to hire strengths and evaluate current employees.

Jack Welch claims to have spent 50 percent of his time assessing talent. This may seem excessive by the standards of the business world, but think about it: How do you build a team with productivity and profit in mind? Make sure that the people working on that team have all the components necessary for success.

The first E in Jack's framework is positive *energy*. We need people who bring positive energy to the room. Doom-and-gloom people are those we refer to as being the "brotherhood of the miserable." They are black holes sucking the life from the room, extinguishing conversation, and dulling performance. We want people who brighten the day and bring a sense of well-being to work, play, and life in general.

The second E is *energizing other people*. A positive outlook and upbeat behavior infect and inspire other people. People with this attitude attract other people—teammates, customers, and managers—to the cause.

Welch's third E is *edge*—the courage to make tough yes-or-no decisions. The world may be gray, but at the end of the business day, is the person willing to provide black-or-white clarity to the team?

Execute is the fourth E—the ability to get the job done. Welch would see Ulysses S. Grant as a high performer in terms of execution. Ultimately, great intentions have to translate into results.

The "1-P" is *passion*. Welch says, "By passion, I mean a heartfelt, deep, and authentic excitement about work. People with passion care—really care in their bones—about colleagues, employees, and friends winning. They love to learn and grow, and they get a huge kick when the people around them do the same." Welch explain that people with passion carry it into all areas of their lives.

The 4-E and 1-P framework is a method of *sorting* people, not necessarily *instructing* them. Rather than attempting to alter nonconforming temperaments, Welch looks for people who exhibit these traits. This approach works for us as well.

SMART MOVE 13
Hire the hungry, not the starving.

Hungry people have a zest and zeal for life regardless of their circumstances. They have a vision for their life and a willingness to work, learn, grow, and put in the time it takes to excel and provide for their families. Starving people, on the other hand, have little vision and a low expectation for their life. They're resigned to a life of mediocrity (or worse), and they quit too soon.

Are you optimistic or pessimistic about your life? Your chances for success, your ability to earn, and your willingness to answer the call on your life all depend on your answer. Are you just hungry for the time being and willing to overcome, or are you resigned to starving for a lifetime?

The "starving" person will continue to starve. He's lost hope in himself, so his only remaining options are luck or divine intervention. Except for his attitude, the starving person is capable, but he continues to look for a handout instead of a hand up.

The "hungry" person has aspirations and ambition. Give her an opportunity and she will run with it. She's motivated to excel and unwilling to settle for her present circumstance. She sees that cause and effect work to her favor more often than not. She'll plan, sustain, endure, and take the long-term view if it is a path to improvement. A hungry person is a profit-maker—a diamond in the rough.

The size of one's bank account or financial statement does not determine whether one is hungry or starving. In my business dealings outside our company, I meet people born into wealth or working in positions of privilege who are not ambitious. It is a tragic waste that could be redeemed by a simple change in attitude.

When we hire a person, we first hire a person's attitude toward himself. That's why we hire the hungry, not the starving. The hungry learn and earn, while the starving complain. We prefer to hire people who are currently employed as opposed to those who are not. These candidates tend to have most if not all the performance dimensions that suit our profile for a successful employee.

SMART MOVE 14
Adopt a rigorous selection process.

Our company's selection process is possibly the most important part of every manager's job. Our continued success is based on our ability to select the right person for the right job—and not just when there is a vacancy to fill.

One of the biggest mistakes made by many businesses is the failure to adopt a standard selection process or tool that is designed to identify and attract those best qualified to do the work. This sounds very basic in principle, but it is typically forgotten during the process of interviewing or selecting candidates for specific jobs.

Too often businesses wait until there is a particular and urgent need to seek out and hire qualified candidates. This is not good for the business or the candidates; it relies too heavily on people who are simply in the right place at the right time—and are not necessarily Right Fit individuals. Our success lies with the *quality*—not just the availability—of the team members who are invited to join us. Thus, we must always be looking for only the best, even if we do not have an urgent need. Hiring "for the bench" gives us the strength to keep our stores staffed with engaged and well-paid team members.

Our selection process is unique in that we are rigorous in our quest for only the best-qualified candidates. If we cannot find what we are looking for in one group, we will simply look for another group of candidates before we make a final decision. We judiciously avoid making what is commonly referred to as "battlefield selections"—those hiring decisions that are made out of necessity, in the heat of "battle." When you select the best, you create a win-win situation for everyone.

CHAPTER SUMMARY

KEY POINTS

- People don't change. Don't try to fix their weaknesses!
- Hire for strengths that fit the job. Understand and manage the many varieties of weaknesses that will inevitably accompany strengths.
- We use the Thurstone Temperament Schedule as our selection tool to help identify the strengths we are looking for in candidates. It is important to have an objective tool to assist in the subjective assessment of candidates.
- We encourage our team members to focus their energy and effort on their strengths and to consistently move away from working in areas where they are weak.

SMART MOVE 12
Win with strengths.

In Jack Welch's book *Winning*, which is read and discussed throughout our organization, he presents his 4-E (and 1-P) framework for building winning teams. We apply it to our talent-identification system in order to hire strengths and evaluate current employees.

SMART MOVE 13
Hire the hungry, not the starving.

Hungry people have a zest and zeal for life regardless of their circumstances. They have a vision for their life and a willingness to work, learn, grow, and put in the time it takes to excel and provide for their families. Starving people, on the other hand, have little vision and a low expectation for their life. They're resigned to a life of mediocrity (or worse), and they quit too soon.

SMART MOVE 14

Adopt a rigorous selection process.

Our company's selection process is possibly the most important part of every manager's job. Our continued success is based on our ability to select the right person for the right job—and not just when there is a vacancy to fill.

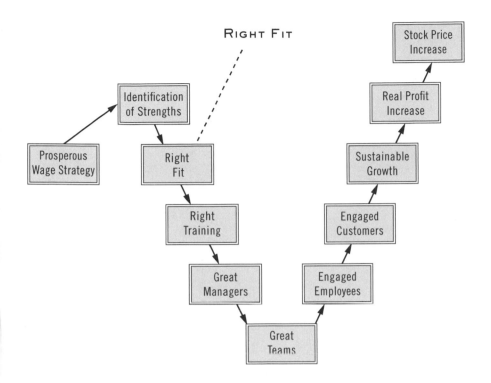

milestones. It follows the logical progression along our Strategic Path: Now it is time to properly position a person for success. Ours is a well-defined, structured strategy for placing talented people who regularly innovate and set new performance records. In turn, this further helps us refine who is a Right Fit and who isn't. It is an upward spiral of constant improvement aligned with our value of learning.

Simply stated, relationships for us are either a Right Fit or a wrong fit—either they conform to standards or they don't. Our ultimate goal is to fully engage people who are totally in tune with our high standards. Is this possible? Yes—but realistically, it is very hard. It is, nevertheless, our goal—we're always working toward *excellence in every role*.

Right Fit involves both performance measures and standards. Standards set the bar, and measures assess proximity below or above the bar.

CHAPTER 4

RIGHT FIT:
HOW DO YOU PLACE THE RIGHT PERSON IN THE RIGHT ROLE?

The effective executive knows that the test of an organization is not genius. It is the capacity to place the person in the right role so that common people can achieve uncommon performance.

Peter F. Drucker, *The Effective Executive*

OUR CONCEPT OF RIGHT FIT IS A MATTER OF PLACING THE RIG PERSON IN THE RIGHT JOB—AND PROVIDING THE PROPER SITUATI FOR THAT PERSON TO BE LED INTO PROSPERITY. Proper incentives, cl expectations, and appropriate measures that accentuate strengths talent are great starters. We want our team members to succeed, per One person's success informs everyone else's expectations and learn We're all developing and improving the company's Strategic Path.

The Right Fit benchmark along our Strategic Path naturally app after the Prosperous Wage Strategy and Identification of Stren

Our standards are upwardly dynamic rather than stationary. You saw that with our personal productivity goal (SMART Move 5). In other words, the Right Fit people naturally raise standards, thereby speeding the identification of talented persons who can successfully exercise their strengths at our company. The reality is, people highly suited to the job make for great performers on the job. Ordinary people do extraordinary work in their Right Fit zone.

Let's say you own a great ⅝-inch wrench. If you have a ½-inch bolt, however, then your great ⅝-inch wrench is of little use. Even though the wrench looks like it's a close fit, it is about as useful as a hammer in that situation. So it isn't about great people but rather about fitness for the job. Each of us is best suited for a certain job. As a result, we're constantly scoping for people who fit the role, can take initiative, and can take performance to the next level.

Fitness for a job is not what many businesses typically measure. Many of our sales associates, for example, were clear and easy choices, as they possessed the correct temperament and the right talent. Some of our most successful sales associates, however, will be the first to admit that they weren't the best students or didn't have the best career paths prior to joining us. They were misplaced along the way and found themselves in positions where the odds were stacked against their success—and getting worse by the day. Background, education, and experience are certainly informative in our hiring process, but these factors are not predictive. Our selection tool, the Thurstone Temperament Schedule (discussed in Chapter 3), along with an assessment of strengths and talents, is far more predictive of Right Fit. In the end, it takes a manager with a gut feeling to size up the fitness of a particular person for the job at hand. The science eventually gives way to the art of hiring.

RIGHT FIT SUITS ALL

Right Fit isn't just about employees. It extends to our customers and relies upon our investors—again fulfilling the trinity relationship of the SMART Moves Triangle.

Our way of doing business attracts certain customers and repels others. We don't attempt to be all things to all people, but we do want to mean the world to our core customers. We serve the underserved, offering them the best customer service available and building long-term relationships. The one-time transactional customer will not value us as the regular engaged customer does. Our cost of doing business with repeat customers is lower because of many factors, including lower risk and less labor. We know that, and we pass along those savings. We work hard for the customers with whom there is a mutual fit and an ongoing relationship.

Investors who grasp our distinctive difference, regardless of whether they come from private equity or public markets, value us more than, for instance, an unsustainable profit-taking day trader does. Our goal is to find investors and lenders who are Right Fits for our company. People who "get it" value what we're doing as a company, both for the people we serve and for the misperceived pawn industry. As our story spreads and pawnshops are understood to be reputable businesses, we expect to attract a broad investment base of loyal support.

COMPANY CHEMISTRY

Good "chemistry" must be a part of nearly every effective team and work group. Right Fit is ultimately a matter of good chemistry. This node on our Strategic Path places remarkable responsibility on managers to select and develop people who align and integrate with a team, our company culture, and our manner of business. When the first three steps on our Strategic Path are performed correctly, it sets up the rest of our Strategic Path to flow smoothly and predictably. If we blow it with the people, then no amount of managing or incentives will remedy the matter.

It's like the wrenches: A ⅝-inch wrench on a ½-inch bolt may get the job done, but the bolt will be stripped as you struggle with the ill-fitting wrench. You'll whack your knuckles with each slip and wear the scars to prove it.

The right person in the right job with proper incentives, striving for excellence, is the single greatest advantage to any organization. As managers, all else we do pales in comparison to this complex assignment of Right Fit.

SMART MOVE 15

Assess performance along a hard line: stay or go.

Assessing Right Fit falls into two broad categories: meeting performance measures and embracing our culture and values. Hard lines are drawn on both of these standards. We have a programmed response to each of three easy-to-understand scenarios regarding performance and values/culture. Performance and values must be in alignment, or changes must take place.

To assess Right Fit in our employees, we have developed a programmed response to each of three easy-to-understand scenarios regarding performance and values:

STAY OR GO?

Scenario 1	Performance plus Values	Stay
Scenario 2	Values but No Performance	New Role
Scenario 3	Performance but No Values	Go

Scenario 1 involves the employee who both meets *Performance* and shares our *Values* and culture. He is a sure fit. *This person stays with us.*

Scenario 2 presents a person who fits our *Values* and culture, but isn't meeting the *Performance* standards of the job. Because employees who fit in with our values and culture are hard to come by, we work with this person based on our newfound understanding of her strengths, seeking to place her into a position where she can flourish. *This person stays, and we change her role.*

Scenario 3 shows a person who meets the *Performance* standards but is running afoul of our *Values* and culture. There is a lot to learn in our culture and manner of doing business, so we work with the person to move him into Scenario 1. If he can't make the transition, however, he is no longer a fit. *This person must go!* We wish him well and then question ourselves about what part of our hiring process failed to catch such a poor fit. A member of the brotherhood of the miserable is never a fit!

We place enormous value on having people who fit our culture. Even a high performer who violates our values is destined for new employment. Success, status, and money can sometimes reveal character flaws. We hire people with strong personalities and egos, who can be challenging to manage; in a culture such as ours, an out-of-control ego will soon be leaving us.

Recently, we fired a sales associate whose attitude of superiority, possessiveness regarding customers, and lack of team behavior were undermining the success of a store. This person could perform on the job like few others, but success went to her head and revealed behavioral problems. We worked with her to stay within the values of the company. Her prima donna approach, however, repeatedly crossed the line. The behavior didn't change, so she had to go.

One person's misbehavior, even if that person is a top producer, can threaten the entire company. No one person is worth that. In this case, the loss of her performance is a small price to pay to preserve the very essence of what holds us all together. In the final analysis, these are actually easy decisions to make, although in the heat of the moment they may appear challenging. This action sent a clear signal throughout the company that our values are very important. Her firing was a positive statement that reinforced our culture.

Right Fit implies the offer of something bigger that one becomes a part of: our business model and company culture as joined by our Strategic Path. While we are exceedingly focused on cultivating the greatness and prosperity of each person in the company, no one person can be above what's right for the company culture. Valuing people means something to our team members—a true connection and pride in being a part of our special company. Right Fit is a beginning, however, not an end. Through the years of training and experience, each person's alignment with the company tends to settle in even more deeply, comfortably, and securely. In the beginning it appears to be a Right Fit, but over time it proves itself to be . . . or not to be.

By keeping winners in winning positions, we all win. *Winning is part of our mission.*

SMART MOVE 16
Implement broadbanding in answer
to the Peter Principle.

Ours isn't an "up or out" company, so we avoid the Peter Principle. "Up or out" is a failed management method because it pushes people out of their Right Fit for the wrong reasons. Our team members don't have to get a promotion to make more money; they can do so by stepping up to another level within their current position.

Our system of developing sales associates produces remarkable results. For a variety of reasons, some aspire to be managers and enter our management training program. Frankly, the profile of a sales associate and a manager are like the aforementioned wrenches—similar in some ways, but they work best on different things. A new assessment of Right Fit takes place. We make it clear up front to the candidate: *If, in the course of manager training, you begin to feel like it is a wrong fit, let us know. Your job as an assistant manager or sales associate joyfully awaits you.* In many companies, the person would be fired. Truth be told, our sales associates are our "rock stars," and our managers are their agents.

"Up or out"—the pressure on an employee to get promoted to the next level or leave the company because he or she is ready for a pay increase—pushes people out of their Right Fit for all the wrong reasons. Our team members can step up to another level within their current position and keep making more money—they don't have to seek that promotion and leave their Right Fit place. "Broadbanding" is the term we use for keeping top performers in their jobs as long as possible and paying them for their excellence and contribution.

All of our sales associates, assistant managers, and store managers hold various titles as a result of our broadbanding for each position. Each of these groups is measured on a timely basis: a weekly review for sales associates and monthly financial and statistical reviews for assistant managers and store managers. In addition to our normal weekly productivity reports, recognition, and celebrations, the top 10 percent of our sales associates earn a special title, bonus commissions, and perks. These rewards are based solely on one's performance relative to peer sales associates, so it is competitive. This fires up our people to strive for excellent personal productivity.

The best of the best—our top twenty individuals out of all sales associates—earn the title of "sales and lending executive" and receive the highest bonus commission payouts. To qualify, a sales associate must be among the top twenty performers for the prior year; he or she then holds the title of sales and lending executive for the entire following year. It includes perks (such as attending the annual managers meeting), a high level of recognition, and celebrations. And our sales executives often earn as much as some assistant managers and managers who work for other companies. The beauty of this compensation arrangement is that an individual does not have to get a promotion to earn more; he or she need only produce more, and the compensation follows. As you can imagine, the people in this group are amazingly competitive and productive. Because it changes just one time per year, these winners have a lot of eager competition.

The next forty sales associates earn the rank of "sales and lending professional" and receive a bonus commission increase over the normal payout. Every quarter, the rankings are reevaluated and recast to show the top 10 percent of sales associates and the new round of sales and lending professionals. There is no resting on one's laurels!

Through broadbanding, top-producing sales associates can earn more than the average store manager does. This negates the need for the "up or out" approach, in which the only path to more pay for talented producers is a promotion that could take them out of their area of strength. Continuity contributes significantly to the profitability of our business.

On the other side of the coin, some sales associates are naturally gifted leaders who are better suited to be managers. Typically, we've picked up on this early in the interview process and have tracked them appropriately toward a desk as a manager rather than a drawer as a sales associate.

Along the way, we have avoided the Peter Principle, which states, "In a hierarchy every employee tends to rise to his level of incompetence." Dr. Laurence J. Peter published this concept in his 1968 book, *The Peter Principle*, to explain the upward, downward, and lateral movement of personnel within a hierarchically organized system of ranks. In short, it reveals that a high-performing individual will attract more and more tasks and responsibilities, until that person reaches a point at which these requirements actually surpass his or her abilities. We seek to avoid and defuse the Peter Principle in order to keep our team members where they can best contribute to the growth of the company—and continue to win.

SMART MOVE 17

Root out the "brotherhood of the miserable."

Employees are either engaged or they are not. Our Strategic Path feeds the engaged and dispels the disengaged.

Office politics, bad managers, toadies, bullies, and pompous asses are not welcome. Ruthlessness is not an acceptable management style.

David Ogilvy, *Confessions of an Advertising Man*

Make no mistake about it: We have a very highly developed business culture in which Right Fit people can expect to win. However, our opportunity isn't right for everyone. Despite our rigorous selection process, sometimes people just don't fit. Our systems are set up to detect and sort out these people: the "brotherhood of the miserable."

I'm not talking about people interested in honest disagreement and debate. No, I'm speaking of constant complainers who always assume the worst. If left unchecked, these people can become negative leaders in the organization and might recruit others into their doom-and-gloom fraternity. We weed them out regardless of their performance. Far be it from us to hold a person back in her search for a more meaningful and fulfilling Right Fit for her life. If our values leave that bad of a taste in your mouth, then why stay and work here? Move on with your life to a Right Fit for you.

If you think this sounds harsh, take another look at the reality. Our company gives each team member every opportunity to succeed. We lay our corporate culture on the table and keep no secrets about our values. It is the individual's choice whether or not to adhere to our system. A person elects to follow either a negative or a positive outlook on life. This parable explains it in a nutshell: A young man struggles to know who he is. Sharing his inner battle with his mentor, he describes his situation this way: "It is like I have two wolves fighting within me. One is moral and good. The other is immoral and evil. I'm torn up inside. I don't know which one will win." The mentor responds, "I do. The one you feed the most shall win."

We strive to identify the "evil wolves" in our midst. Gallup's employee engagement survey helps us to discover actively disengaged employees—or as I call them, "corporate terrorists." And they must be fired! Like members of a sleeper cell, they actively work against the company, often using passive-aggressive techniques. This minority can't be ignored and must be reengaged or aggressively removed as one would remove a threatening cancer.

The chart below is a recent Gallup employee engagement survey for our company. Our disgruntled members are clearly identified as the small percentage at the bottom of each column; membership in this group has dropped from 6 percent in 2005 to 5 percent in 2006 and 4 percent in 2007. In comparison, 15 percent of the general U.S. working population is "actively disengaged." And note the percentage of employees on the top of each bar: While fully 70 percent of our workforce is "engaged," only 28 percent of the U.S. workforce claims to be so.

The number of engaged team members continues to grow with our company. The ratio for 2007, shown above each bar on the chart, can be read this way: For every one member of the brotherhood of the miserable, we have 17.5 highly engaged employees. Comparing our measures to those of the U.S. working population standard used by Gallup clearly demonstrates the remarkable ratio of our employees who are actively engaged in their work.

WORLD CLASS EMPLOYEE ENGAGEMENT PERFORMANCE

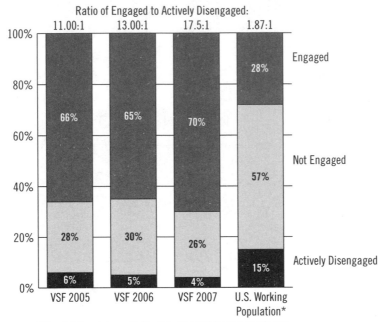

Ratio of Engaged to Actively Disengaged:

| 11.00:1 | 13.00:1 | 17.5:1 | 1.87:1 |

*Compiled from data provided by Value Financial Services records and files along with data from other sources including Gallup.

SMART MOVE 18
Recruit full-time employees only.

We have no part-time employees; only full-time dedicated employees work with us. Part-time employment leads to a lower level of commitment or even a divided sense of loyalty than is the case with a fully engaged employee. Thus, our practice is to hire only full-time, dedicated employees who are engaged in what they do and how they do it.

I say, therefore, that the arms with which a prince defends his state are either his own, or they are mercenaries, auxiliaries, or mixed. Mercenaries and auxiliaries are useless and dangerous; and if one holds his state based on these arms, he will stand neither firm nor safe; for they are disunited, ambitious, and without discipline, unfaithful, valiant before friends, cowardly before enemies; they have neither the fear of God nor fidelity to men, and destruction is deferred only so long as the attack is; for in peace one is robbed by them and in war by the enemy.

Niccolò Machiavelli (1469–1527), *The Prince*

This excerpt from Machiavelli's most famous work on politics is often applied to business theory in the modern world. He makes the case for hiring only full-time, fully dedicated employees rather than mercenaries (part-time warriors). Because their loyalties lie elsewhere, he argues, mercenaries fight (if they fight at all) for a cause different from that of the fully engaged, full-time, dedicated soldier. The same argument can be applied to today's workforce, which is the reason that our company doesn't employ on a part-time basis.

Down the road, some number cruncher might question our Prosperous Wage Strategy. He would put forth a "brilliant" proposition to increase profits by firing the highest-earning associates and replacing them with lower-wage and part-time employees. However, this profit-taking move would gut the company of its culture, crush employee morale, and undermine earnings. Our Strategic Path would be plowed under, and soon we would see major profit losses that far outweigh any short-term gains.

By now, you have a sense of our selection process, our mutual commitment, our investment in our team members, and the expectation placed upon every person in our company. Practically speaking, accepting anything less than full-time employment would undermine the long-term viability and standing of our employee and customer engagement—and thus, our profitability. Even the hint of part-timers is so removed from the context of our way of business that it would be a threat to our very existence.

SMART MOVE 19

Conduct regular reviews of every employee.

People like to know where they stand. This can involve very difficult discussions that both manager and employee may prefer to avoid. Avoidance, however, is not a worthy management method. To ensure that every employee knows where he or she stands, we have adopted a systematic approach: the quarterly file review. At least four times each year, the manager and the reporting team member meet to confirm that there is a Right Fit. Is the person getting the full advantage of what we have to offer in terms of growth and earnings? Is the company receiving the full contribution this person can give to his or her personal productivity and team?

The quarterly file review refines the mutual understanding between manager and sales associate of strengths and Right Fit for the role. Managers ask, "What does this person bring to the table in the way of productivity and customer service? Based upon what I know, would I hire this person again?" Each review is a discussion centered on strengths and talents (not weaknesses) to determine where the team member can be the most productive and engaged in his or her role. We avoid the futile frustrations, wasted time, and expensive process of "fixing" weaknesses and focus instead on strengths (SMART Move 12). The focus is on helping the person soar within his or her natural abilities.

Quarterly file reviews assess every employee's performance, fit, and history every ninety days. Meanwhile, one-on-one reviews for all team members happen every four weeks to regularly provide each employee with current and actionable information. New hires receive 30-, 60-, 90- and 180-day reviews. This combination of reviews allows us to catch challenges and opportunities quickly—plus the employee knows where he or she stands. Thus, if the quarterly file review results in a dismissal, no one is overly surprised.

These small cuts from time to time create healthy turnover (SMART Move 2) and reinforce right performance. The review process also allows for a rigorous and timely human resources approach to our business as opposed to a ruthless approach of across-the-board layoffs. Candid, objective reviews are the highest-impact method managers can use to preserve and advance our culture and performance level.

SMART MOVE 20

Believe that there are no unimportant jobs.

Every job is important. This means that at any successful company, there are only important people in important roles. It is management's responsibility to instill worth in each employee's job in order to deliver this feeling of importance.

Gradually and without knowing it, we are revising all of our opinions on the subject of high wages. There is no reason, for instance, why a garbage collector should not be a first-class employee.

Henry Ford, *Today and Tomorrow*

When Florida had a run of hurricanes in 2004, broadcasters told government workers that offices were closed for nonessential personnel. What kind of language is this? I would certainly dislike having my job labeled "nonessential"—the implication being that the job really doesn't make a difference.

There should be no such thing as a nonessential job. In our company, there are no unimportant jobs. Every position requires specific strengths than can only be best performed if the person has the talent and is the Right Fit for the job.

People are the strategy. When every job matters, management takes the time to set expectations, measure by them, select the right person, and hold that person to performance standards. Not only is this approach incredibly good for business, but it also sends a message to all team members that their work matters, their engagement efforts are worthwhile, and they are making a difference with their lives. Every job at our company is important—or the position would not exist!

The entrance into employment here is admittedly a very narrow door, but once inside the company, every employee has access to a great expanse of opportunity, because we view the relationship as one that can last a lifetime. Against this long-term backdrop, every new person hired is expected to be another winner in the making. We train, reward, and celebrate our team members like the hand-selected members they are—and we make sure to communicate that sense of value to every one of them. In this sense, they are an elite corps of nonelitists.

SMART MOVE 21
Promote an egalitarian versus an elitist approach.

Our egalitarian approach to business is based on beliefs that are deeply rooted in the inherent dignity and equality of a person regardless of one's station in life, society, or our company. This view applies to our employees, customers, and investors alike. Contrasting this is an elitist view—an "us" and "them" perspective—reminiscent of a caste-based social system. This "holier than thou" attitude is ultimately a form of degrading others in order to place oneself above them.

The best way to test a man's character is to give him power.

Abraham Lincoln

Regardless of our customers' socioeconomic situations, we are careful not to become elitist. We are conscious of the trap of inflating self-worth at the expense of another human being. Therefore, we actively promote egalitarian ideals, both preventatively (to avoid perpetuating elitism) and prescriptively (to eradicate existing elitism). The root value of this is kindness.

Do egalitarianism and Right Fit appear contradictory? They aren't. Egalitarianism views people as inherently equal, regardless of situation or circumstance. While they may be *equal in worth*, Right Fit reminds us that people are simply not *the same*—each is suited for a particular task, job, or mission. The common ground goes back to using a person's unique strength as the basis of hiring; every person has a measure of greatness.

This understanding is fundamental to our corporate culture. That said, the rise to management along with the adoption of others under your charge reveals character. Any manager runs the risk of losing sight of this core value and breaking away from one broad type of manager—the egalitarian—and toward the other broad type, the elitist.

An elitist thinks he is better than the next person, particularly if that person is in a reporting position to him. Elitists will see my role as CEO and place my worth as a person above that of a store manager. Certainly my position, responsibility, and authority are superior in this context, but the store manager is no less important. This isn't about job understanding, fit, or direct performance. It is about one's attitude toward one's fellow man. Elitism at its core is the basic disrespect of another person. In business, it is a disaster waiting to happen; it always leads to failure if left unchecked. Elitists run off good employees and undermine customer relationships. This results in unhealthy turnover. Experience tells me that people who need to put down others in order to build themselves up eventually tear down and damage everything—the team, the store, and company performance.

The firing of Arthur Blank and Bernie Marcus from Handy Dan Home Improvement Centers blindsided them. Feeling like middle-aged has-beens, they used their unkind experience to invigorate themselves into starting The Home Depot. These two men ended up reinventing a retail category. Kindness scarred with pain and embarrassment must have shaped their approach to employees in the founding of the company. They realized that clueless do-it-yourself homeowners need to be treated as a person, not talked down to by some home repair expert. At The Home Depot, very experienced and well-trained employees dispense advice, hope, and encouragement along with lots of products needed to do the job right. Bernie and Arthur advanced the Prosperous Wage Strategy and built an empire of stores.

In contrast, Bob Nardelli, the briefly tenured, highly chronicled former CEO of The Home Depot, brought an elitist approach to this retail operator's employees, customers, and investors. His initial strategy was to replace high-paid, long-tenured employees with part-time employees with an eye to increasing profits. He rode the brand equity, but eroded the company culture and profit-making ability of the people. Sales predictably plummeted as the implication of his short-term profit-taking strategy was realized. In May 2006, the company's annual meeting was a token thirty minutes long and Nardelli ignored shareholder questions. This wasn't strategy; it was elitism run wild, played out in a series of rude acts and disregard for people. And The Home Depot has paid the price: Its loss of market share has been the gain of Lowe's Home Improvement Centers.

Elitists have great difficulty with the principle of fairness. At the root of fairness is the basic respect of another person, which is the foundation for integrity, honesty, and direct dealings with others. Elitists typically ruin things they run—or at least take away all the fun. We describe elitists as people who "just don't play well with others."

Egalitarian managers, however, rarely miss a beat in their relationships, because they respect people and don't play power games. Our managers accept power with grace, showing their true character; they don't get hung up on status or title. They help team members learn and excel in the service of customers. Neither their position nor the authority goes to their head. The egalitarian manager seeks to understand those with whom he or she works, never assumes he or she has all the answers, and genuinely seeks the opinion of others. Respect of the other person is given freely, even in disagreement. Egalitarian managers leverage people's potentials and strengths, rather than exploiting their weaknesses as the elitist does.

Egalitarians are by nature kind people—and the kind of people we hire and promote.

SMART MOVE 22
Expect excellence in every role.

Excellence in every role is a corollary to SMART Move 20, "Believe that there are no unimportant jobs." While that SMART Move sets a minimum standard, excellence in every role raises the bar across the company.

With every job an essential one that contributes to the overall success of the company, it stands to reason that we expect excellence in every role. Regardless of whether one is on a store team or the headquarters team, we measure performance according to our definition of excellence on the job.

This isn't just corporate speak. The value excellence holds for us reflects our commitment to securing the best fits in the right roles and to rewarding right actions and behaviors. Staffing every job with the best talent provides a positive and challenging workplace filled with innovation, fun, and constant growth. Excellence begets more excellence. It serves to both attract and retain Right Fit people. Ultimately, our attitude about excellence brings strategic advantage to every line item on the income statement, in every phase of the business, and throughout every fiber of our company culture.

CHAPTER SUMMARY

KEY POINTS

- Assuming you have talented people, the only matter of importance is fitness for the position. A hardworking person in the wrong position is bound to fail. On the other hand, a person who is a Right Fit is more apt to excel and succeed.

- Right Fit is a concept applied to employees, customers, and investors alike. We have the greatest control as applied to employees. The assessment of an employee's fit within our company is therefore of major importance to the ultimate growth and performance of the business.

- Right Fit substantially improves the potential for success. Wrong fit undermines profits and our company culture.

- If your staff includes members of the "brotherhood of the miserable," fire them!

- People in the wrong fit need to move to where they are a Right Fit.

SMART MOVE 15

Assess performance along a hard line: stay or go.

Assessing Right Fit falls into two broad categories: meeting performance measures and embracing our culture and values. Hard lines are drawn on both of these standards. Performance and values must be in alignment, or changes must take place.

SMART MOVE 16
Implement broadbanding in answer to the Peter Principle.

Ours isn't an "up or out" company, so we avoid the Peter Principle. "Up or out" is a failed management method because it pushes people out of their Right Fit for the wrong reasons. Our team members don't have to get a promotion to make more money; they can do so by stepping up to another level within their current position.

SMART MOVE 17
Root out the "brotherhood of the miserable."

Employees are either engaged or they are not. Our Strategic Path feeds the engaged and dispels the disengaged.

SMART MOVE 18
Recruit full-time employees only.

We have no part-time employees; only full-time dedicated employees work with us. Part-time employment leads to a lower level of commitment or even a divided sense of loyalty than is the case with the fully engaged employee. Thus, our practice is to hire only full-time, dedicated employees who are engaged in what they do and how they do it.

SMART MOVE 19
Conduct regular reviews of every employee.

People like to know where they stand. This can involve very difficult discussions that both manager and employee may prefer to avoid. Avoidance, however, is not a worthy management method. To ensure that every employee knows where he or she stands, we have adopted a systematic approach: the quarterly file review. At least four times each year, the manager and the reporting team member meet to confirm that there is a Right Fit. Is the person getting the full advantage of what we have to offer in terms of growth and earnings? Is the company receiving the full contribution this person can give to his or her personal productivity and team?

SMART MOVE 20
Believe that there are no unimportant jobs.

Every job is important. This means that at any successful company, there are only important people in important roles. It is management's responsibility to instill worth in each employee's job to deliver this feeling of importance.

SMART MOVE 21
Promote an egalitarian versus an elitist approach.

Our egalitarian approach to business is based on beliefs are deeply rooted in the inherent dignity and equality of a person regardless of one's station in life, society, or our company. This view applies to our employees, customers, and investors alike. Contrasting this is an elitist view—an "us" and "them" perspective—reminiscent of a caste-based social system. This "holier than thou" attitude is ultimately a form of degrading others in order to place oneself above them.

SMART MOVE 22
Expect excellence in every role.

Excellence in every role is a corollary to SMART Move 20: "Believe that there are no unimportant jobs." While that SMART Move sets a minimum standard, excellence in every role raises the bar across the company.

CHAPTER 5

RIGHT TRAINING:
HOW DO YOU TRAIN YOUR TEAM MEMBERS?

All men are not voluntarily intelligent; they must be taught. All men do not see the high escape for drudgery in work by putting intelligence into work; they must be taught. All men do not see the wisdom of fitting means to ends, of conserving materials (which is sacred as the result of others' labours), of saving the most precious commodity—time; they must be taught.

Henry Ford, *Today and Tomorrow*

THE AMERICAN DREAM IS ALIVE AND WELL AT OUR COMPANY, BUT AS FORD WOULD SAY, "IT MUST BE TAUGHT." That's why we annually invest an average of forty hours of formal training for every team member, in addition to constant on-the-job training. Our Prosperous Wage Strategy isn't the end of the opportunity; our Strategic Path is just the beginning of what's possible. Prosperity in its many forms is available

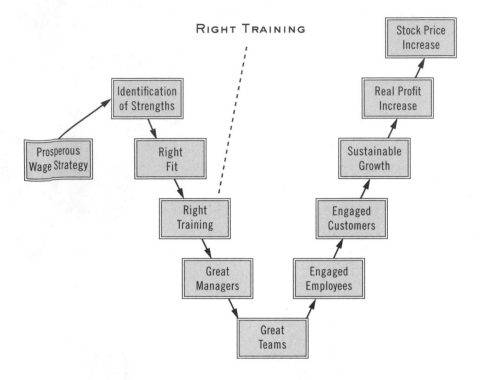

RIGHT TRAINING

here to any team member. If prosperity is the promise to team members, then Right Training is the fulfillment of that promise.

Ingrained in the human spirit is a desire to excel, make a difference, and be recognized and rewarded for one's performance. What makes the United States of America a great nation is the freedom to pursue and reap the rewards of one's legitimate labor. U.S. citizens and immigrants share the hope of providing a better life for their families through the dream of opportunity, wealth, and home ownership.

Yet pursuing the American Dream is fraught with frustrations and challenges. Small business ownership statistics reveal huge failure rates. Corporate America can provide a job and benefits, but too often a person's spirit is crushed by tight boundaries, limited upside, office politics, and disincentives to excellence.

The object of our training system is to release and channel talent. Our team members are entrepreneurially minded individuals in pursuit of the American Dream. Each team member is trained to run a business from his or her drawer. Each manager is trained to run a business generating more than six figures monthly. Each region leader is trained to supervise managers and oversee a multiunit business grossing up to $10 million per year.

Right Training does not overcome inherent flaws in the business equation or in a leader's thinking. Retailers in particular are notorious for paying low wages. This sows problems right at the start. Does one really have to speculate on why the retail sector generally shows such rapid turnover, unchecked pilferage, poor customer service ratings, repeated business failures, lost earnings, and absenteeism? (Just look at the difficult histories of such companies as Circuit City, Sears, and The Home Depot!) Great training produces a real return on investment; when the opposite path is followed, the negative results are made plain for all to see.

To say that our training begins on Day One of a person's employment would be misinforming you. In fact, our training begins from the first moment a prospective employee touches our company as a customer, as an attendee at a job fair, as a visitor to our website, or in a myriad of other ways. Our interviewing process begins our orientation process. Even if the person doesn't get hired, he or she may end up referring a friend or associate who is a better fit for our team.

Once employed, every new team member goes through three days of formal orientation to learn about our company and how to operate in our business. In addition to this, employees receive an additional forty hours of training in diamonds and jewelry during their first year. This amount of up-front training is almost unheard of in the retail sector. Throughout their careers, team members will experience a combination of formal and informal training on an ongoing basis.

One of our core values is to promote a culture of learning so that every day we get better at what we do. Again, this isn't lip service. Our formal training is systematic, programmed, and under constant improvement; its success is measured by our financial results.

Training is that part of learning and communication in which managers are freeing people's strengths and feeding their talents, so they can reach their full potential. Yet management's efforts can go only so far. Invariably, peer learning is the greatest source of everyday training. When one team member helps another, they both learn. Our teams are our best source of ideas, innovation, and training. Our stores are the true learning laboratories of up-to-date training. The challenge is to facilitate the rapid dissemination of these improvements throughout our operations. In management, we're actually collecting and packaging the best SMART Moves from the store level and communicating these throughout the company. No one person claims ownership of these ideas! What matters is what works.

Regardless of whether our growth takes us to Geneva, Florida, or Geneva, Switzerland, we bring the American Dream to deserving team members. Our Strategic Path is a blueprint to prosperity. It connects the dots for the trinity relationship—employees, customers, investors—so the three are in fact acting as one. And yet prosperity takes many forms, not just financial. With Right Training, self-worth and net worth can be synergistically aligned to produce a healthy prosperity that informs, inspires, and fuels our team members to even higher standards.

SMART MOVE 23
Send employees to a Company Learning Center.
Strategic Management Awareness and Resource Training Camp, or SMART Camp, is the name of the training program for all managers, all headquarters team members, and select other individuals. Its programs contribute to employee engagement, customer satisfaction, and shareholder value.

SMART Camps are four-day events that combine training, updates, feedback, book reviews, social events, celebrations, and camaraderie. This is our company's version of General Electric's Crotonville training center. About twenty-five people attend any given SMART Camp each month; attendees are from a cross-section of the company. Over the course of a year, every director of operations, store manager, assistant store manager, and manager-in-training will attend SMART Camp.

Each month's group is large enough to be diverse, but small enough to create real relationships and allow for meaningful discussions. Tables are set up in our meeting room to form a large, open rectangle, so everyone can make eye contact; participation is encouraged. SMART Camp attendees are clustered by tenure, with training delivered appropriate to their progress on the learning curve. SMART Camp 101 is for team members with us one year or less; 201 is for those two years on the job; and 301 is for team members with three years or more experience. Headquarters personnel also attend these training sessions.

The typical agenda for the 101 level of SMART Camp is as follows:

> **Day One:** Opens with a companywide overview by the CEO. Typically, our senior management team is present. This is an open and honest presentation—an update on our financial performance, operations, and personnel. Any questions and other topics are welcome. We then hold a book review (SMART Move 24), in which specific small groups have been assigned chapters to present to the group. This interaction enhances engagement.

> **Day Two:** We dedicate this day to specific skills training, as applicable to each group's personal or professional development. We follow this with a group social event, where attendees can interact and get to know people from other stores.

Day Three: Attendees tour local stores to observe and learn about cleanliness, service, and merchandising. After lunch, there's a discussion of what was observed and what could apply at this or that store. This day is always capped off with a group dinner.

Days Four and Five: More skills are taught, as appropriate to each group's tenure and challenges. This is followed by discussions and operational updates, with key members of senior management returning to close this SMART Camp session.

What is the value of SMART Camp? Although the functional and operational costs of a SMART Camp session are expensive, it remains one of the best investments in our people because the returns on smart, hardworking team members pay dividends in the length of their employment. This is an activity in holding the company together with leadership and culture. SMART Camp is smart business, as it builds our team members' business skills, forms relationships, and promotes our company culture. All of this contributes to employee engagement, customer engagement, and shareholder value.

Other levels of SMART Camp include advanced training for operations and loaning techniques. There is also specific training about how to schedule time and activities by using various tools that we make available to our people. These SMART Camps are very dynamic, and we change and update them as needed.

SMART MOVE 24

Build business intelligence with book reviews.

Reviews of business strategy books are our secret weapon for team building. They cross-pollinate relationships and ideas, and develop confident and learned leaders in our profession. Each review is a team presentation done with fun and learning in mind.

Advance preparation for a specific book review is part of each participant's commitment to SMART Camp. The typical book review takes place on Day One of SMART Camp with a facilitator who knows the material to be discussed. This is a group activity; each attendee presents one or more chapters of the selected reading material.

Presenters are encouraged to share their impressions of the material and point out at least one particular "takeaway" from their section of the book. Once the presenter has completed his or her discussion of the assigned material, the facilitator opens the floor for comments and discussion. Discussions are directed by the facilitator toward how the information can be useful to team members in the course of their day-to-day activities.

These energetic learning events range from basic oral reports to PowerPoint presentations to skits. Occasionally, two or more presenters will discuss the material as a team effort and present accordingly to the group. This part of the SMART Camp schedule promotes team building and is a great "get acquainted" session.

To be in the room during book reviews is typically a great time. Fun, however, does not lose out to functionality and learning. Invariably, the insights and understanding gleaned from the books directly reinforce our methods and solidify team members' thinking. Many truly great ideas and improvements are birthed from these book reviews. The best way to get everyone on the same page is to read a book. To this end, many of our managers conduct in-store book reviews using the books from SMART Camp.

Over the years, we've settled on the following books for the first three years of SMART Camp:

- SMART Camp 101 reads *First, Break All the Rules*, by Marcus Buckingham and Curt Coffman. This book describes what the best managers do and how they break away from conventional wisdom.

- SMART Camp 201 reads Jim Collins's book *Good to Great*. At this point, attendees are well versed in our culture. This book thrusts strategic and systems thinking into their business psyche in an attempt to get them working smarter. Our Strategic Path comes even more to life.
- SMART Camp 301 reads *The 7 Habits of Highly Effective People*, by Stephen Covey. Now attendees are competent in almost every phase of the job, so the goal is to get them to focus on themselves.

Book reviews offer many benefits in addition to the content within the covers. Employees have told me countless times that they hadn't read a book since school, and because of SMART Camp they're now reading books constantly. Book reviews are the best team-building activity that I have ever experienced. It often leads to comparing notes and informally sharing the good books we've read recently. This SMART Move engages learning that spills into all areas of life.

We often assemble a group of people who have been identified as being promotable to participate in special book reviews. Included are classic business reads from the likes of Henry Ford, Peter Drucker, and Tom Watson. These books expand our high reachers' vision of business and understanding of what we're all about.

Our Strategic Path is etched into the hearts and minds of our team. Every book review inevitably reinforces what our people know to be true about our way of conducting business. Another frequent comment we hear is, "The author says to do such and such, and here we're already doing that." Sometimes, individuals disagree with the author, and other people are quick to weigh in. Book reviews build confidence and create context within our company. People gain perspective and realize that the big boys have nothing over us. Wrestling with some of the best business thinking available energizes and engages our team.

Readers are leaders. There's no two ways about it. Learning pulls the mind up out of work, opens it to new possibilities and fresh thinking, and reinforces positive behaviors. None of us are perfect, but that shouldn't prevent us from improving every day, at every turn. Accessing the wisdom of great thinkers in books is like mining for gold: Nuggets of treasure inevitably come to light.

Book reviews are indeed our secret weapon for team building, cross-pollinating relationships and ideas, and developing confident and learned leaders in our profession.

CHAPTER SUMMARY

KEY POINTS

- According to Henry Ford, all elements of efficient and productive work must be taught. This means training is essential for a business to be profitable.
- Our company considers training an investment, not an expense. Training along our Strategic Path leads to prosperity for employees, customers, and investors alike.
- People must be willing learners and they must share what they have learned from success as well as failure.

SMART MOVE 23

Send employees to a company learning center.

Strategic Management Awareness and Resource Training Camp, or SMART Camp, is the name of the Value Financial Services monthly training program for all managers, all headquarters team members, and select other individuals. Its programs contribute to employee engagement, customer satisfaction, and shareholder value.

SMART MOVE 24

Build business intelligence with book reviews.

Reviews of business strategy books are our secret weapon for team building. They cross-pollinate relationships and ideas, and develop confident and learned leaders in our profession. Each review is a team presentation done with fun and learning in mind.

CHAPTER 6

GREAT MANAGERS: *HOW DO YOU BUILD SUCH CONSISTENCY OF PERFORMANCE THROUGHOUT THE COMPANY?*

I believe it is not harder to build something great than to build something good. It might be statistically rarer to reach greatness, but it does not require more suffering than perpetuating mediocrity.

Jim Collins, *Good to Great*

MANAGERS ARE THE LEVERAGE POINT IN OUR PEOPLE STRATEGY. They are the source of our present and future performance. Nothing is a more powerful producer and predictor of profits than manager continuity and turnover. We monitor, measure, and report these statistics monthly through the entire chain of our management team, all the way to the board of directors. "Great Managers" is more than a label in a box on our Strategic Path; they represent an intense standard of excellence that

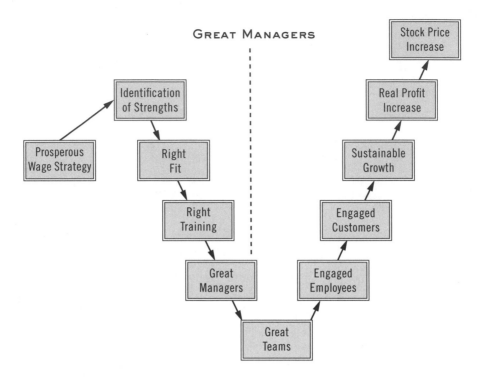

is the cornerstone of the team concept. Most of all, this milestone on the Strategic Path is about the individuals who lead and manage stores to success—small business "owners" whose personal efforts collectively form the results of our company.

Each manager leads a profit center called a "store." Our managers run the store, build the team, extend our company culture, and produce results. Managers are the difference between *good enough* and *great*. "Individualism" is promoted as our style of management. In essence, that means managers are allowed to treat each person differently, to push their appropriate buttons to achieve results.

Great Managers may be seen essentially as "people alchemists" who successfully transform the base talents of those in their charge into skills that produce golden profits . . . and more. They bring out the best in people, it's true—but their work isn't magic. It's science and art joined on our Strategic Path to create the best working experience for a highly select, properly placed, well-trained, and meaningfully engaged team member. All this translates into a tremendous customer experience that raises our reputation, brand loyalty, and profits. Managers are local masters of prosperity.

Great Managers help team members transform their natural talents and raw strengths into high productivity and profitability. Great Managers show team members how they make a difference for customers and, in turn, are rewarded by enjoying the fruits of their labor. What could be more important?

GATEKEEPERS TO OUR FUTURE

Research has taught us that people don't leave great companies; they leave bad managers. If there's a turnover problem in a business and an ineffective selection process has been ruled out as the cause, then look to your managers. When we have a store with lots of turnover, then we have a problem with a manager. However, we don't leave it all on the shoulders of our managers. Leadership is often said to be lonely; that's not the case here. Each manager is individually backed and supported by a region leader, our director of operations, and the headquarters team.

Identifying, hiring, training, and cultivating Great Managers, therefore, is the top priority of our people strategy. Our *management candidate pool* is the system we use to raise up our next generation of managers. As you might expect, managers benefit from our Prosperous Wage Strategy. We identify certain strengths (somewhat different from those of a sales associate) in search of a Right Fit, and then we provide Right Training to produce Great Managers. This is a two-year process, but it works. The first year a manager is in that role, he or she produces more than $375,000 in store-level net income. Here's the reason why: Ninety percent of our managers are hired with the intention of making them managers, while only 10 percent come from the ranks of our assistant managers or sales associates. Because of their particular temperament, managers are better suited than the typical sales associate for leading people. The same is probably true of the differences between the managing real estate broker who runs a business and the agent who runs the roads with clients.

Managers have an innate capacity for administration, people development, and effective controls. Still, individuals who manage within our team must be vetted, trained, and tested before earning the opportunity to run a multimillion-dollar store. Though marked for a manager position, most management candidates typically start their tenure by learning to be exceptional sales associates. They learn our business firsthand, gain a high appreciation for our customers, and acquire unparalleled knowledge about every type of store transaction.

In addition to becoming competent as a sales associate and proficient in each role in a store, each management candidate must develop a prescribed series of set management-related skills and experiences. Throughout the process, the candidate is regularly observed by a full complement of on-site mentors: an assistant manager, a manager, and a region leader. I directly oversee and constantly monitor the performance of individuals in the management candidate pool. Every month I review these measures and deliver a "Turnover and Continuity Report" to our board of directors; these statistics are leading indicators of our near-term and long-term profitability.

All this preparation precedes any individual being named manager of an individual store. By giving candidates time to learn, mature, and gather experience, we're building confidence and competence. It's like a guild system with apprentices, journeymen, and masters—except we call them assistants, managers, and region leaders. Developing from within over time is our best option if we're to build sustainable profits.

FIRST THE PERSON, THEN THE TEAM

Brownie Wise, the innovator of the Tupperware home party system in the 1950s, said, "If you want to build the business, build the people." With due respect to Brownie, I'll modify that statement to say, "If you want to build the business, build the managers." The concept of building *people* is too broad and overwhelming from the company's point of view, so we focus on raising managers who in turn raise the team.

We're acutely aware that we're in the business of transforming everyday people into everyday winners. Our stores provide a platform that enables us to train, challenge, and assess how well each team member is progressing and profiting. As the team members grow, so do the benefits to our customers and investors. This is the essence of sustainable profit making. It has taken a long time to get the profit-making engine fully operational. Now that it is, we're constantly under the hood fine-tuning it.

Our managers are the primary coaches who help their store staff members to more fully realize and engage their great potential. This isn't hype; it's a huge part of our strategy. Most people are taught to overcome weaknesses. As described in Chapter 3, we teach our managers to do the opposite by building on strengths and managing *around* the weaknesses. Because it supports both managers and employees throughout this process, our Strategic Path gives us a massive competitive advantage in this respect.

For decades, great leaders such as Tom Watson, Jr., and Henry Ford and thinkers such as Peter Drucker have asserted the strengths approach to people development: to hire people for their strengths and compatibility for the role. To love one's work is a massive strength. As we teach a team member how to more consistently function in strengths and to manage around weaknesses, that person matures into his or her own life. Because getting better every day is a core value, our team members are amazing in their ability to eventually self-manage to success within our framework.

We hire fine men and women whom we believe have the potential to work here for a lifetime—and they have to believe it, too. Our training, oversight, and standards tell us whether that turns out to be the case. We are a top-performing, demanding, highly structured, fast-paced place to work. People burn out, and this costs the company a great deal of money every year. That's not good, but it is better than keeping underperformers who will cost us even more dearly down the road by undermining our productivity and eroding our ethics and culture. Those who leave us, nevertheless, never leave empty-handed. Most are enriched by the personal growth and insights learned during their time here. They depart as better people and are better positioned to succeed in finding a Right Fit situation for their strengths.

Our Strategic Path is useful to any business where true teams are desired, especially in the retail segment where individual store leadership is desired. Our method and principles can only work, however, if top leadership invests in and commits to the strategic thinking and essential design of our Strategic Path; this is how we bring the company culture to life. Admittedly, it is a complex work akin to unraveling a ball of twine wrapped in many types of string: emotions, business, preferences, and disciplines. Nonetheless, our way remains far superior to the alternative: the top-down command-and-control methods of many corporate hierarchies. Freedom is a powerful advantage when a business is competing for the hard work of employees who will best serve the customers, making all sales and profits possible.

INDIVIDUALISM

In many businesses, a manager's day is spent bringing people up to minimum standards of conformity based on a set of rules, policies, and procedures from the company manual. In our opinion, the manager's actual role should be that of a business coach helping each person deliver his or her best performance. Imagine how a Great Manager must feel, knowing the right people are in the right roles. We set our managers free from "policing"; the goal instead is to release each person's strengths for maximum performance. This type of relationship forms a remarkable bond of authentic trust built over time, as between player and coach. It is a more mature posture toward management, and those who succeed at it deserve the black belt of management talent and temperament.

Promoting individualism requires an extraordinary set of circumstances and managerial talent. Our Strategic Path is the essential road map for creating the right conditions for people to thrive. For example, a manager has to trust the sales associate with the stated objectives and must be willing to let each person find his or her particular way toward meeting the weekly personal productivity goal. This would be hard for most managers, who assume that "management" means "Do it my way." Individualism is a matter of trust, a willingness to let people succeed (and sometimes fail) as they discover their way of success. It is a fitting alternative to the conformity and overbearing control of a "my way or the highway" management approach.

Complicating matters is the fact that individualism at times may appear to be unfair because it allows for flexibility in the way managers deal with different employees. Ironically, however, it may be the most fair of all management styles. Rather than forcing all the square pegs into round holes, a Great Manager makes sure that each team member has the opportunity to focus on his or her strengths—sometimes by tweaking the situation or making small allowances for a better fit. This is intended for the mutual benefit of the employee, the team, and the company—not to mention the customers and investors, who benefit from happy and productive employees. A manager is in essence custom-fitting each team member with the feasible cultural and performance norms, while also providing ample maneuvering space for

engaging, meaningful, and rewarding. Team members look forward to coming to work with one another and with the customers.

SMART MOVE 25
Create limits on span of control.

"Span of control" refers to the number of reports a manager has in his or her charge. Across the board, our span of control is narrower than that practiced in the marketplace. This allows for a high level of interaction between team members and team leaders. The smaller-than-typical span of control allows us to be proactive instead of reactive. Also, there is more time for training, inspection, and profit-making.

The learning curve effect and relationship value are amplified, with the financial payoff being much greater than if the span of control were wider. A first-level multiunit manager (region leader), for example, has no more than five reporting store managers. This means the region leader is in every store at least once a week for a day. Every team member has direct access to his store manager and the store manager's boss, the region leader. Questions are to be asked of the managers and will be asked by the managers. This places time and energy on profits in the place of being in a constant urgency mode. If one is overloaded with too many stores they tend to only have time to put out fires.

SMART MOVE 26
Discover the benefit of long-term training programs.

The manager of a store first has to understand what it means to be a manager. All our managers train in the sales associate role. They have to learn the business from the ground up.

Schools were set up for salesmen—the training course now runs as long as eighteen months.

Thomas J. Watson, Jr., *A Business and Its Beliefs*

Mastery of the all-important frontline functions is essential to earning and holding the respect of the store team. We don't expect our management candidates to be sales associate superstars, because they're wired differently. But this training time (eighteen to twenty-four months) builds their understanding of the business, credibility with their teammates, and appreciation for the people they will one day manage. Great Managers have a genuine appreciation for the frontline operational realities faced by the sales associate and customer, because they've walked in a sales associate's shoes as part of their training.

SMART MOVE 27
Create a lease line.

A *lease line* represents a commitment between team members and the company: When team members cross that line, they are there to perform and the company will protect them from the outside world.

Each one of our stores has a *lease line* that is identified by a prominent yellow strip painted on the threshold of each store. The concept of the lease line is very real to all team members, as it represents a commitment: When they cross the lease line, the company will protect them from the outside world; in return, however, they must be totally focused on performance.

Great Managers enforce the lease line—in both directions. They make sure that it works for our employees but also that our employees live up to the accompanying requirements. We feel that our team members should be free of any outside influences when they report for work, and every effort is made to help them maintain this productive environment. They are there to perform; the primary focus is on the customer. It's showtime: time for our team members to provide exceptional customer service and, at the same time, to earn a great living for themselves and their families.

Reporting a bit earlier than scheduled is a common practice among our team members, as they want to be ready to start when their shift starts. Reporting to work while consuming food or completing their dress for the day is *not acceptable*. Once a team member crosses the lease line, our open culture of trust and accountability begins. Outside distractions are not welcome.

The lease line idea is a well-known practice and a much appreciated part of our company's culture. In exchange for a positive and supportive work environment, engaged team members welcome the opportunity to come to work ready to serve our customers and earn a great living. Over time this concept has proven to be a win-win solution for everyone.

SMART MOVE 28
Play chess instead of checkers.
Practice individualism. Know that each team member has success with his or her own specific moves, much like in the game of chess.

Too often, managers assume every player moves in the same direction. But a skilled chess player knows many moves are necessary to capture the prize. Likewise, successful team members have a variety of moves they call into play each day while serving our customers. It is this variety that allows them to earn compensation well above the average for a similar position in other companies, while providing exceptional customer service as measured by the Gallup Organization.

Our managers play to the various strengths of each team member and are quick to recognize that different people react in different ways to the same situation. Unlike a game of checkers, where most anyone can figure out the next move, our team members serve customers as if they are a part of a game of chess. Every move is customized to the customer and the needs of that customer. That is why our company consistently outperforms all other multiunit operators in the industry: We play chess instead of checkers. This is yet another win-win for everyone, customers included.

SMART MOVE 29
Build bench strength.
Having bench strength means that we have depth of personnel in every position. The best defense against any kind of turnover is to always have a capable replacement prepared. Others might think of this as being "overstaffed" or having too many talented people vying for the same position. On the contrary, bench strength softens the blow of losses and increases gains.

Eagles don't flock; you find them one at a time.

Ross Perot

Our selection and training are so rigorous that we hire the right people when we find them, not just when there is a job opening. If we're hiring only when there's an opening, then we're already too late. When it comes to staffing, leaving positions open will create more holes. Creating bench strength means that when an opening happens, we can put a well-trained individual in a store and hardly miss a beat.

"Bench strength" is a concept we've borrowed from sports and applied to employee recruiting, team productivity, and company growth.

Unlike a sports team, however, we're not limited by a roster size, because career growth and opportunity abound as we expand regionally, nationally, and internationally. We're building teams, for sure, but we're really building a *league* of winners.

Cut to the sideline scene of a professional football game, where you see a young quarterback and the veteran with a clipboard in hand, discussing plays. The best teams instill a spirit of bringing up the next generation of top performers. On one hand, they are training their competitors; yet on the other hand they know bench strength makes for better overall team results should someone go down injured. True professionals welcome healthy internal competition because it spurs performance to even higher personal levels. That means the rewards and awards will follow—for all.

Bench strength seems counterintuitive to many businesspeople. They fixate on protecting turf instead of growing it and expanding the range of opportunity. They are not focused on getting better every day. A mind-set of abundance can be learned, but it takes time on the bench to trust that the system and the people really do have your best interests at heart. Once it becomes clear that our system works to the greatest advantage of all parties, even the most wary individuals can accept and embrace our methods. A vision of tomorrow lived out authentically today helps the strong realize even greater strength in relationships.

SMART MOVE 30
Calculate the cost of turnover.
Employee turnover is the most expensive unreported cost of any business. That's because it's hidden in a number of different places. In some ways, you can never fully calculate the cost, because the ripple effect touches every line on the income statement. However, you can estimate the cost for each person lost at one times that person's annual pay.

Although stated earlier, Frederick F. Reichheld's comments about retention rates are worth repeating.

> In most of the industries we've studied, the companies with the highest retention rates also earn the best profits. Relative retention explains profits better than markets share, scale, cost position, or any of the other variables usually associated with competitive advantage.
>
> **Frederick F. Reichheld, *The Loyalty Effect***

In 2008, we produced total revenues just over $130 million and $18 million EBITDA. With our employee turnover of 25 percent and an employee base of 700, we replaced 175 individuals during the year. There are many ways to calculate the individual cost of turnover, but the generally accepted formula is one times annual compensation for the person who is leaving. At an estimated cost of $40,000 per person, this means we missed potential earnings of $7 million. This figure does not even represent the total loss, as turnover affects every line on the income statement.

The average businessperson or investor doesn't perceive employee turnover as that costly. Ignoring the cost, however, doesn't make it go away. We assess the full implication of turnover because it keeps us focused on what matters most: valuing people.

Fortunately, we're a profitable business that can absorb the insidious cost of turnover. Much of my day, however, is invested in solving the challenge of turnover. The lower our turnover, the more a whole lot of other problems take care of themselves.

You may be wondering how employee turnover costs can be calculated and where the income statement is affected. This partial list is just a start.

- People-related costs
  - Hiring costs—recruiters, job fairs, advertising, screening, interview time

- Training costs—employee time, materials, facilities, time away from the job
- Payroll and benefits costs—wages, health insurance, workers compensation, retirement
- Higher payments into state fund (a result of higher rate in unemployment ratings)
- Management and staff time in damage control

- Operations-related costs
  - Decisionmaking
  - Sales
  - Cash drawer overages and shorts
  - Inventory shrinkage and loss
  - Cost of goods sold, repairs, cleaning, returns
  - Facilities—care, cleaning, and upkeep

- Supply costs

- Opportunity costs (affecting both current year and net present value)
  - Lost sales—less experienced persons and lost relationships
  - Less upselling
  - Loss of customer goodwill (particularly spread by word of mouth)
  - Promotional costs
  - Team rebuilding instead of fully functional
  - Increased staffing costs
  - Less time for customers because of administrative issues

Perhaps this list will stimulate your thinking and give a sense of the scale and scope of turnover costs. Our Strategic Path provides an excellent means to systematically reduce turnover and improve loyalty, clearing the way for our managers to become Great Managers.

CHAPTER SUMMARY

KEY POINTS

- Managers are the leverage point of our people strategy. They represent the integration of performance and culture that affects the customer experience and investor returns.

- Management continuity—time at the same store location—is the best predictor of a store's profitability and capacity to outperform competitors.

- Managers are gatekeepers to future performance. They are the frontline alchemists who transform our workforce into productive team members.

- According to Gallup Consulting, people don't leave great companies; they leave bad managers. Therefore, we hire people specifically for our management track or our sales track. There is very little crossover.

- Individualism is like tailoring. Within reason, Great Managers attempt to fit each employee's needs, strengths, and condition to the unique situation within the store. This allows each store to achieve top performance.

SMART MOVE 25
Create limits on span of control.

"Span of control" refers to the number of reports a manager has in his or her charge. Across the board, our span of control is narrower than that generally practiced in the marketplace. This allows for a high level of interaction between team members and team leaders. The smaller-than-typical span of control allows us to be proactive instead of reactive. Also, there is more time for training, inspection, and profit-making.

SMART MOVE 26
Discover the benefit of long-term training programs.

The manager of a store first has to understand what it means to be a manager. All our managers train in the sales associate role. They have to learn the business from the ground up.

SMART MOVE 27
Create a lease line.

A lease line represents a commitment between team members and the company: When team members cross that line, they are there to perform and the company will protect them from the outside world.

SMART MOVE 28
Play chess instead of checkers.

Practice individualization. Know that each team member has success with his or her own specific moves, much like in the game of chess.

SMART MOVE 29
Build bench strength.

Having bench strength means that we have depth of personnel in every position. The best defense against any kind of turnover is to always have a capable replacement prepared. Others might think of this as being "overstaffed" or having too many talented people vying for the same position. On the contrary, bench strength softens the blow of losses and increases gains.

SMART MOVE 30
Calculate the cost of turnover.

Employee turnover is the most expensive unreported cost of any business. That's because it's hidden in a number of different places. In some ways, you can never fully calculate the cost, because the ripple effect touches every line on the income statement. However, you can estimate the cost for each person lost at one times that person's annual pay.

CHAPTER 7

GREAT TEAMS:
HOW DO YOU BUILD YOUR TEAMS?

When you ask people about what it is like being part of a great team, what is most striking is the meaningfulness of the experience. People talk about being part of something larger than themselves, of being connected, of being generative. It becomes quite clear that, for many, their experiences as part of truly great teams stand out as singular periods of life lived to the fullest. Some spend the rest of their lives looking for ways to recapture that spirit.

Peter Senge, *The Fifth Discipline*

GREAT TEAMS ARE THE BASE POINT OF OUR STRATEGIC PATH—BOTH LITERALLY AND FIGURATIVELY. All the prior steps—all our work and investment—point to the development of not just teams, but Great Teams. That means a store team lives up to its potential financially, socially, and culturally from each group's perspective: employees, customers, and investors. As the bottom point on the check mark of our

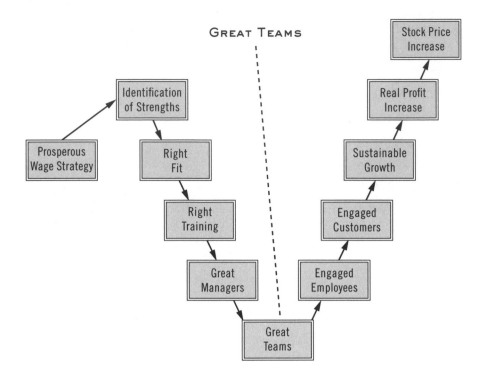

Strategic Path, this milestone indicates that the investment is complete and the return on investment is about to begin.

Many companies talk of teams and teamwork, but it's just lip service. Our company is committed to having a Great Team in every store. It isn't enough to have a fully staffed store; that just means we've filled positions. Teamwork really matters in our stores because of the camaraderie, challenge, and pace of the work. It wasn't difficult for us to figure out that we needed a system to help us merge individuals into workgroups, to transform workgroups into teams, and to make teams into Great Teams.

One of the truly Great Teams in our company is headed by store manager in Orlando, Florida. This store is alive and energetic. This manager has been with us for ten years and she's just twenty-eight years old. She's risen through the ranks and now heads a highly disciplined and productive team with deep-seated values. People who work in that store love one another. She has done everything right; with our help, she has selected her team members with science and has held them together with leadership and culture. Everyone on the team is a Right Fit. The eighteen team members divvy up work so that each is working from his or her strength. On their own initiative, they gather every Monday morning as a team to say a prayer for support in meeting their productivity goals, to care for one another's needs, and to intercede for customers' needs. They pray for the prosperity of all those with whom they come in contact. They are guided by a vision; quite simply, it is to be the best and to live life to the fullest.

For our company to be a great one, uniquely Great Teams must abound throughout our stores and headquarters staff. Great Teams, however, are rare experiences in the life of the average person. One of the reasons is the rareness of Great Managers. The impression, therefore, is that Great Teams are a matter of happenstance and luck rather than good planning and managing. Admittedly, a measure of good fortune is involved; but it is a measure of luck, not a mountain, that makes the difference.

We're unwilling to settle for the impression that Great Teams are fleeting and fragile flashes of brilliance that require a certain alignment of the planets and stars. Consider the "dynasties" in the world of athletics, such as John Wooden's UCLA college basketball teams or the New England Patriots of NFL football led by Bill Belichick. There is always a Great Manager at the helm with a system of team development and the tools required for longevity. Players on Great Teams come in and out of the lineup, yet performance remains world-class.

We're intentionally building a company of Great Teams—one in every store is the obvious goal. Great Teams are not built by accident. It requires thought, design, intention, and patience to develop a corporate culture that is capable of consistently producing at the highest potential level for every store in the chain. We set out to become our industry's most profitable organization worldwide, measured the only way that matters: on a per store basis tied to return on investment. From that starting mission, we've toiled upstream to figure out what works.

This is an intense effort along a marked course: our Strategic Path. The process is subject to vulnerabilities and variables capable of undermining the goals of our Great Teams. That's life. We're focused on progress, not perfection. Just because something is difficult doesn't mean we shouldn't pursue it with excellence. Challenges, problems, mistakes, and errors are all lessons that we can use—learning cloaked as failure but still holding seeds of greatness.

Fortunately, with so many "lessons" over the years, we've actually failed our way into success! That's largely because we've been willing learners. Counter to what one might believe, the more we've failed, the more we've learned. Our "tuition" has been paid—but we go back to school every day anyway. We continue to learn and to benefit from our education. Over time this competence has made our business that much easier, more profitable, and more fun.

GREATNESS IN AMBIDEXTERITY

"Corporate culture" is one of those buzz phrases casually tossed about in business and academic circles. Here are a couple of definitions from dictionary.com:

- The philosophy, values, behavior, dress codes, etc. that together constitute the unique style and policies of a company.
- The shared values, traditions, customs, philosophy, and policies of a corporation; also, the professional atmosphere that grows from this and affects behavior and performance.

I take no exception to these definitions. Corporate culture, however, has an inherent problem. The science and art of managing corporate culture is underdeveloped and misunderstood by many line managers. Many managers discount the role of culture in business in favor of management controls and systems that are typically grounded in managerial accounting and industrial engineering. Corporate culture is easy to ignore, but to do so is sheer folly. It is like a right-handed person using this dominant hand for everything they do. It might work and be the best you've got, but to use only one arm just doesn't make sense when you have two. Corporate culture has for too long been the nondominant hand; many organizations have simply allowed it to atrophy. But greatness in this case cannot be one-handed. Greatness requires a meaningful alignment and integration of the business model and the corporate culture. Our Strategic Path achieves this.

Great Teams are a matter of discipline. This discipline is aligned to a stated strategy that's anchored in a meaningful purpose, a clear vision, a defined and measurable mission, and values that govern behaviors. Great Teams look, feel, and function differently than the average team does, because two hands are better than one. Our Strategic Path encourages ambidexterity with regards to managing corporate culture and business performance.

Chapter 14 explores our corporate culture more fully—in particular, how attracting the best people leads to consistency and success—so you will come to understand both "hands" of our company. We're true to our understanding of what makes our Great Teams successful, though we're not rigid or righteous about it; if we've learned anything, it is that there is always a better way of getting things done. We can't let our success create contentment or arrogance.

For example, every book review we conduct (SMART Move 24) is geared toward the question *How does it help us cultivate greatness?* Frankly, that's a team effort. Great Managers realize that the further they get from the front lines of the business, the more they risk becoming disconnected from the day-to-day reality of what is happening with the customer. It is the team that knows what's working and what isn't. On the other hand, senior managers are able to sit back and be more reflective; they can see trends across the company by connecting dots not necessarily observed by a store manager. Only with both perspectives can our teams achieve greatness.

DID WE WIN THE GAME TODAY?

One may get the impression we're creating robotlike conformity when it comes to everything and anything having to do with our business. But the fact is, we're dealing with hundreds of entrepreneurial personalities. Each person possesses a heightened need for adventure and expression, but structure and focus are also required. Our corporate cultural norms and operational policies ultimately provide a sufficiently comfortable berth between freedom of expression and accountability to cultural norms and productivity standards.

For example, managers are free to operate their store in a way that best serves the local neighborhood. They conduct their own promotions. Meanwhile, they are required to conform to safety and security requirements. They must follow our Green and Clean cleanliness program. They practice our hiring standards. Strict corporate guidelines in some areas of the business work alongside local rules in other areas to give our managers and sales associates sufficient independence mixed with adequate external checks and balances. This ensures success yet still encourages the entire store team to take initiative and to think innovatively.

Within our collective cultural norms and commitment to the mission of profitable performance, there is a great deal of diversity among managers. Yet for each and every one of them, profit is the scorecard at the end of every business day. Each store team can answer the question, did we win the game today? In our case, the box scores—our daily and weekly personal productivity goals—tell the tale of individual and store performance. Based on these results, we learn from our losses and grow from our gains, so we are constantly improving.

THE FLOW OF CORPORATE CULTURE

Corporate culture is generally a ghostlike mystery for businesspersons. Its existence and influence are undeniable, but its elusive and indeterminate nature defies controls. When compared to the more immediate, tangible "hard skills" of accounting, controls, and operations, corporate culture makes even marketing look like a hard science. Instinctively, managers default to the hard skills that seem to more readily contribute to profit production. Also, for most managers, the hard skills are easier to master because they're inanimate and static. People are messy, moving, and unpredictable.

So how do we make sure our managers are "ambidextrous"—trained to use both "hands" appropriately, rather than relying too heavily on one hand or the other? How do we ascertain when our company culture is being tainted by wrong fit or wrong attitudes? And how can we be certain that managers balance local practices with our centralized values?

First of all, it's clear that we have a very strong culture within our company. Each store reflects the company culture *as well as* the individual leadership style of its manager. The difference in local store culture is more a matter of style and personality than a substantive variance from the company culture. As discussed in the previous chapter, employees leave managers—not companies. Each manager must develop a working environment and style that works for the team and the location. Therefore, the most important culture for team members is always the local store culture. Our managers are ready students, eager to adapt to and embrace our culture as it exists within their location.

Let's think of corporate culture as a flowing river of philosophy, values, behaviors, dress, and so on. The river springs from the core strategic statements of purpose, vision, mission, and values. The mouth of the river flows to a sea of customers in the form of daily transactions. The river's length can be compared to all the steps of our Strategic Path covered thus far. Each SMART Move is a tributary that adds to the flow.

When the river is flowing clean, clear, and strong, then the customers are satisfied. River debris or pollution impinges the customer experience and chokes the flow of profits. Attempts to remove and treat the pollution at the river mouth are remedial at best because the upstream pollutants continue to flow. The mouth is typically the most expensive and least effective place at which to fix the problems. It is, however, where the problem is most apparent, so it tends to garner the one-handed manager's attention and action. Customer service training, team-building events, and time management courses are investments often made to modify behaviors and provide relief at the mouth, but these efforts do not get upstream. SMART Camp and book reviews (SMART Moves 23 and 24), on the other hand, are activities that take place upstream, so they have positive results downstream.

Symptomatic of these problems is the cry of many a modern employee: "We're expected to do more with less." They are expected to stem the stream of unending problems that dock at their desk; they're left with ownership of the problem simply because they're the last people downstream. Within their scope of authority, they can only do so much, so they learn from their upstream counterparts, do the best they can, and pass the problems on to the customers.

We who lead need to do our job of managing upstream to permanently solve pollution problems. In other words, we have to look back along the prior steps of our Strategic Path to the brooks, streams, and creeks—to discover what's flowing into the river of our culture and affecting our performance and psyche. We must be sure that the intended spirit—the mission, values, and standards on which the company is based—is being upheld across all facets of the organization.

What is the value of the spirit of a company? It's a difficult question to answer for most business leaders, but a positive or negative value must be assigned. A strong, productive corporate spirit alone does not make a company profitable. It will, however, accentuate the positives and allow the company to realize its greatest potential. One need only look at the "best in class" in any industry—Southwest Airlines, Publix, Chick-fil-A, Wells Fargo—to understand the value of spirit in a company.

Rivers of water are measured by physical survey. The flow of a culture, however, is akin to an intangible asset that is not on the balance sheet—but is ultimately reflected in revenues and profits. Like goodwill, corporate culture can't be touched or visually inspected, but it can be surveyed. Enter Gallup Consulting and its world-class survey methods and observations.

In 2003, Gallup was first engaged to assess the "purity" in the flow of our company culture. According to Gallup, our company morale is off-the-chart positive, productive, and supportive within our highly competitive and energetic workplace. Prior to that time, my gut told me that we were healthy, but I had no third-party metrics to confirm my beliefs. The words of Henry Ford, Tom Watson, and Peter Drucker had predisposed me to focus on corporate culture, but it was Gallup that provided the best tools and statistical basis for assessing the intangible character of culture.

Our profits and productivity beat our competitors by multiples. The normal competitor benchmarks one might use are actually irrelevant. We're left competing with ourselves, and frankly, this makes me proud of our team members. And now, thanks to team, employee, and customer surveys conducted by Gallup Consulting, we have measures and methods instead of hunches and hopes. We have proof positive that team spirit is an invaluable accelerant to our performance. Today, our culture survey results and metrics are as important to running our business as our financial statements are. Thanks in large measure to our Strategic Path, the waters and shores for the river of our corporate culture is well charted and managed.

From this vantage point, let's turn to our Strategic Path in light of corporate culture. In the accompanying illustration, specific nodes are labeled "Pre-Corporate Culture" and "Corporate Culture" and are shown with respective arrows and numbers to identify sequence.

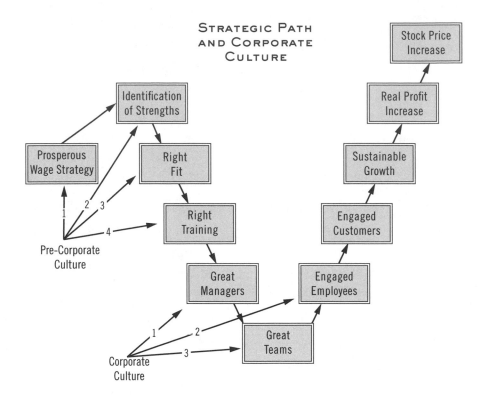

STRATEGIC PATH AND CORPORATE CULTURE

Pre-Corporate Culture is the upstream tributary feeding company performance. As its name implies, it precedes the existence of corporate culture. There is no mystery to this; it's a simple matter of cause and effect. The strategic source is fed by tributaries of SMART Moves and flows into the course of Prosperous Wage Strategy, Identification of Strengths, Right Fit, and Right Training. The desired effect is a culture of greatness: Great Managers, Great Teams, and Engaged Employees. The results seen in the realm of Corporate Culture, therefore, are mostly formed upstream in the realm of Pre-Corporate Culture, and are then experienced through managers and the team that they create (or fail to create).

Every step of Pre-Corporate Culture along our Strategic Path is essential to building greatness. Any compromise travels downstream and creates added costs, burdens to the business, and accumulated debris for the employees. Yet when performance suffers, the natural inclination for typical managers is to address the issue directly at the point of the problem. There's obvious merit in this apparent remedy when it comes to employee-specific matters. But for *patterns* of problems (such as turnover), it won't do to clean the river at the site of the problem; the fact is, more pollution is on the way from upstream. Temporary fixes may work momentarily, but they're doomed to eventual failure. In such cases, employees have been set up unintentionally to fail; they are in fact taking the fall for leadership, which has neglected to design and manage the corporate culture that will produce Great Managers and Great Teams. The lesson here is that remedial work on the problem has its limitations when the real source of the problem lies upstream in Pre-Corporate Culture. In short, if the plan is to fix problems at the mouth of the river, then the managers are too late; they are merely playing catch-up.

Forming and transforming a culture is mostly an upstream matter of making many SMART Moves, all of which feed into the flow of our Strategic Path. If a management team is in constant crisis at the mouth of the river, however, upstream management may appear to be an unaffordable, nearly impossible undertaking. Understandably, when the city at the mouth of the river is flooded with trash and pollution, beginning upstream remediation is a hard sell. Nevertheless, leaders have to make bold investments or else the crisis will always prevail. Our Strategic Path charts an essential series of locks and dams so the company culture can flow cleanly and productively.

THE CORPORATE CULTURE BLUEPRINT

When the Army Corps of Engineers works a river project, they have blueprints. The entire design and construction team—the general contractor, project manager, supervisors, and construction workers—is able to refer to the plans for direction and guidance while remaining unified. Similarly, our Strategic Path is the blueprint for building a great company culture. It frees the entire workforce to do their jobs according to set standards while still functioning within individual strengths.

In our blueprint, the milestones that belong to Pre-Corporate Culture are the upstream work for the Corporate Culture section. Compared to work at the mouth of the river—where Great Teams and Engaged Employees meet our customers—these elements are hidden from the view of those who don't understand our system. There's some lag time between an upstream improvement and a downstream result. It can be years before a positive change is seen, if at all. Many factors come into play, so accurately measuring initiatives is challenging. The gauges are not so precise nor, frankly, so popular or publicized as traditional financial measures are. Practically speaking, the immediate rewards for investing in long-term foundational improvements appear to hurt short-term results. This tension, however, is healthy and dynamic.

When the short-term mind-set goes unchecked, the business climate rapidly unravels into a series of quick fixes designed to manipulate current financial performance rather than build sustainable performance. There are a multitude of ways for managers to manipulate short-term results and performance goals to gain pay bonuses. That's unhealthy for the employees, customers, and investors. Left unchecked, every aspect of the business will take on a shabby appearance physically that reflects a deeper problem in the planning and thinking.

In contrast, a manager with an expectation of remaining in the same store has incentives to think in the long term and to make the kind of investments needed to fix the upstream issues. Herein lies an important reason for keeping our managers in the same location year after year: continuity. This subtle but vital shift in psyche is tied directly to the manager's commitment to a particular store. Continuity does away with short-term thinking, quick rewards, cutting corners, and passing problems on to the next manager. According to our company culture blueprint, our managers can expect longevity in *their* store. They can't pass problems along to a stream of managers coming along behind them; there isn't supposed to *be* a next manager. Our managers live with their decisions, and suffer the consequences or enjoy the rewards. This keeps them real about the business fundamentals and invested in having a Great Team. The blueprint of our Strategic Path, along with constant learning, provides a means to build a strong store culture aligned with the company culture. Confidence builds competence, which builds more confidence—and so the upward spiral rises to new heights.

What makes all this so entertaining is that we don't know just how much our managers can grow a store. Consider the fact that our managers who have five years or more in the same location deliver store profits 300 percent better than our best competitors' average stores. And, collectively, they keep raising the bar to new heights. Truly, they have unlimited upward potential and are rewarded for their sustained and increasing performance.

Managing the length of a river of activities, as opposed to making modifications at the mouth, appears to be a daunting challenge. Without a blueprint, it is nearly impossible to build and sustain results on a large-scale basis across many teams. Managers with the right blueprint who are trained and rewarded for right behaviors thrive in this system. Once managers are trained and understand our Strategic Path, it becomes their essential navigational device as they form their store culture. Most will admit they didn't know how to manage company culture before they were introduced to our Strategic Path. It wasn't that they couldn't manage; they just didn't know how to manage culture, except instinctively.

Individuals inclined toward management can apply this basic competence to most anything they're asked to manage. Their talent and skills make them capable of collecting data, making analyses, and preparing for a return on investment. True managers like and trust people. If you cannot trust, you cannot manage other people. We train managers to focus on controls *and* culture. Right Training helps them to become Great Managers who build Great Teams because they function with both hands.

There's a reason why our first-year SMART Camp book reviews (SMART Move 24) start with Buckingham and Coffman's book *First, Break All the Rules* and are followed in year two by Jim Collins's *Good to Great*; these classic studies of leadership provide essential insights for creating a blueprint that works. Our corporate culture blueprint—our Strategic Path—is an amalgam of improvements by many bright, talented, and hardworking people, combined with lessons from thought and business leaders past and present.

THE CIRCLE OF GREATNESS

Many a business leader aspires to achieve greatness with their companies. Regardless of their definition of *greatness*, oftentimes success is all too elusive and these individuals settle for just being average or pretty good. The billion-dollar question to greatness has always been how. Even Collins talks about the "black box" where an unexplainable "special something" happens.

Greatness, regardless of how one defines it in one's own industry, is found at the base of our Strategic Path; it is marked by the circle labeled "Corporate Culture." To build a great company, one has to build a great culture to spawn growth and enhance productivity. Show me an unkempt corporate culture, and I'll show you a company that is underperforming its annual earnings, profit, and contribution to society *by at least half*. Meanwhile, if there is a "secret" to this greatness, it lies in the circle labeled "Pre-Corporate Culture." It is sustained and reinforced in the culture and designed into the business model.

Since the beginning our goal was to be a truly great company. To improve our company culture, we've sought the world's best thinking from the last two millennia and broadly assimilated it to our requirements. We've benefited greatly from Gallup's research and findings by building upon and modifying these, as well as folding in the contributions of others and spicing it with our own perspectives. The result? We are a company of Great Teams.

SMART MOVE 31
Calculate your return on hiring.
Wrong hires are investment losses. Right hires produce an ongoing stream of income, resulting in a positive rate of return. While the costs of recruiting, selecting, training, and payroll are generally very predictable, the return on hiring is not as easy to predict.

The first five points on our Strategic Path represent our investment in team members. We want to know their strengths, place them correctly, and grow them through training. Yet even this isn't enough; after all these steps, it still takes a Great Manager to turn their talent into gold.

Why make this significant investment? The entire length of our Strategic Path shows the answer. Let's split the check mark vertically down the middle, with Great Teams resting on the centerline. We're left with two halves—a left and a right side—as shown in the accompanying figure.

The left side represents the investment we make in people. The right side shows the return on that investment in terms of profits, goodwill, reputation, brand, customer loyalty, and (ultimately) shareholder value. The left side is the cause; the right side is the effect. Therefore, wise investments in the cause side of our Strategic Path more predictably produce the effects that generate true wealth.

Let's put the humanity aspect of hiring aside for the moment and speak in pure financial terms. The return on a good hire is an "infinite positive"! The negative return on a bad hire, on the other hand, is

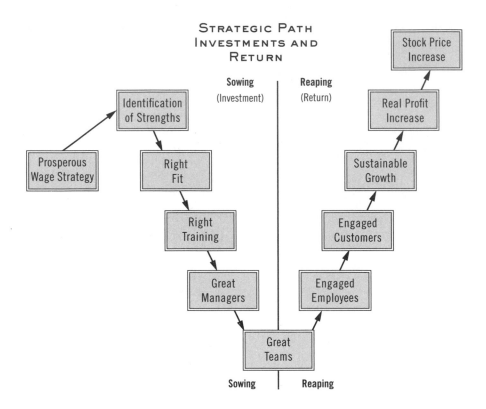

STRATEGIC PATH
INVESTMENTS AND
RETURN

at least one times that hire's annual compensation, plus hidden costs that can appear on every line item of the income statement. The chart below shows the average performance throughout the first four years of a great hire's "life cycle":

AVERAGE RETURN OF A GREAT HIRE

Timeframe	Productivity
Year 1	$650,000
Year 2	$790,000
Year 3	$850,000
Year 4	$950,000

The return on a great new hire clearly grows year after year; the potential for growth is infinite. Compare this to the cost to the company of a bad hire, according to the best estimate possible for the effect on every line of the income statement:

annual compensation × number of turnovers in one year = cost of a bad hire

$$\$40,000 \times 175 = \$7,000,000 \text{ per year}$$

By calculating a company's return on hiring in this way, it becomes clear how important it is to be very particular about hiring only those individuals who you're reasonably sure will contribute to a Great Team.

SMART MOVE 32
Live the Golden Rule.

The Golden Rule is *Do unto others as you would have them do unto you.* There is a deeper message here: We are to understand others as individuals and respect their thoughts, ideas, and input. The Golden Rule sets forth the tension between privilege and duty. A greater understanding of this great law of life inspires and invites us to raise the standards of our character, offer grace and understanding to others, and see the world through their eyes.

No executive has ever suffered because his subordinates were strong and effective.

Peter Drucker, *The Effective Executive*

Albert Einstein said that the most important question any human being can ask themselves is, is this a friendly universe? Einstein challenged us to draw a line in the sand—to look within our hearts and make a decision about how we are to treat one another. Our universal view is either friendly or unfriendly. Our viewpoint colors our lives, one way or the other.

Great Managers all over the world have very little in common when you explore their backgrounds, experiences, and styles of management. What they share, however, is remarkable: They treat everyone the same by treating them differently, and they always remember that little kindnesses and courtesies are so important to human interactions.

Being kind and treating others with respect and dignity also pays dividends in terms of loyalty and engagement. One of the reasons our team members are so engaged, according to the Gallup Organization, is the way managers treat them.

Coach Lou Holtz, in his book *Wins, Losses, and Lessons,* describes the kind of culture we encourage. Early in his career, Holtz shares, he learned that for one person to win, someone else doesn't necessarily have to lose. It is human nature for people to take an interest in those who are interested in them. In fact, helping other people get what they want often leads to getting what *you* want. People may not always remember what you gave them or what you did for them—but they'll remember how you treated them.

SMART MOVE 33
Be wary of roast beef issues.

New people bring fresh perspectives and opportunities for questioning what's working and what isn't. Managers who answer a person's question with killer phrases like "That's the way we do things around here" arrest learning and growth. At our company, little is sacred except constant learning and improvement.

We don't want tradition. We want to live in the present, and the only history that is worth a tinker's damn is the history we make today.

Henry Ford, *Today and Tomorrow*

In a culture of learning and improvement, there is no place for what we call "roast beef issues." Here's the story behind this amusing term that our company has adopted:

The Roast Beef Story

Shortly after a young couple was married, the husband observed that his bride always cut off the ends of expensive top sirloin roasts prior to placing the meat in the roasting pan. The cuttings were tossed away, as the young bride had no use for these small but expensive end cuts.

One day, the young husband asked his wife why she always cut off the ends of the roast. She replied that her mother taught her to do this. He suggested that they call her mother to find out the reason for this practice, which seemed unusually expensive and wasteful to him.

The young bride called her mother, who replied that she was not sure; her mother had taught her how to cook a roast. The young bride then called her grandmother to further inquire about their family practice.

"Grandma," she asked, "why do you cut the ends off a roast before placing it in a roasting pan?"

Grandma replied, "When your mother was growing up, my roast pan was too small for the length of the roast, so I cut off the ends and put them aside for later use. This way, I could make the roast fit in the pan. Why do you want to know?"

"Roast beef issues" are those questions that your average manager might answer with "That's just the way we do things around here." At our company, we use this term to prevent us from getting locked into ways of doing things that no longer make sense. Instead, if someone questions something, let's ponder their point of view. Our team members are smart; perhaps this individual is presenting a valid insight or an opportunity for innovation or education. It is important to know the *why* of ways and not just the *how*.

All management meetings should include an opportunity to question our practices, reports, or anything that might come up during discussion. We constantly search for easier and more productive ways to conduct our business. Every action, thought, and practice is open to being scrutinized, discussed, and improved—by anyone.

We are always willing to listen and consider new methods of improvement and growth. There is no pride of authorship. Any theoretical or operational approach can be changed in a flash. We subscribe to a notion of Henry Ford's: that when policies of the past are shown to be inadequate for the needs of the future, we must be willing to make a clean break and start anew. The importance we place on this open learning approach serves us well.

CHAPTER SUMMARY

KEY POINTS

- Stores are really teams of people. The longer they work together and learn to work as a team, the greater is their expected productivity and profitability.

- Workgroups and teams are different. Workgroups are a collection of people working in close proximity. Teams are workgroups that function as a coordinated unit. Continuity helps to create a team within our company culture.

- The development of company culture (the "Corporate Culture" section of the check mark) is preceded by our "Pre-Corporate Culture"—the first four steps of our Strategic Path.

SMART MOVE 31
Calculate your return on hiring.

Wrong hires are investment losses. Right hires produce an ongoing stream of income, resulting in a positive rate of return. While the costs of recruiting, selecting, training, and payroll are generally very predictable, the return on hiring is not as easy to predict.

SMART MOVE 32
Live the Golden Rule.

The Golden Rule is *Do unto others as you would have them do unto you.* There is a deeper message here: We are to understand others as individuals and respect their thoughts, ideas, and input. The Golden Rule sets forth the tension between privilege and duty. A greater understanding of this great law of life inspires and invites us to raise the standards of our character, offer grace and understanding to others, and see the world through their eyes.

SMART MOVE 33

Be wary of roast beef issues.

New people bring fresh perspectives and opportunities for questioning what's working and what isn't. Managers who answer a person's question with killer phrases like "That's the way we do things around here" arrest learning and growth. At our company, little is sacred except constant learning and improvement.

CHAPTER 8

ENGAGED EMPLOYEES: HOW DO YOU KEEP YOUR EMPLOYEES SO SATISFIED AND PRODUCTIVE?

I believe the real difference between success and failure in a corporation can
be very often traced to the question of how well the organization brings out the
great energies and talents of its people.

Thomas J. Watson, Jr., *A Business and Its Beliefs*

A BUSINESS ASSOCIATE AND I WERE HAVING LUNCH AT HIS SUGGES-
TION IN A LOCAL MEXICAN RESTAURANT. He had frequented this place
for more than two decades. When our waitress approached the table,
she said, "Hi, hon! Haven't seen you in a while."

"You're right. It's probably been a year," he said. "You've got a good
memory for customers."

"You've been coming here as long as I can remember," she smiled.
He asked, "How long have you worked here?"

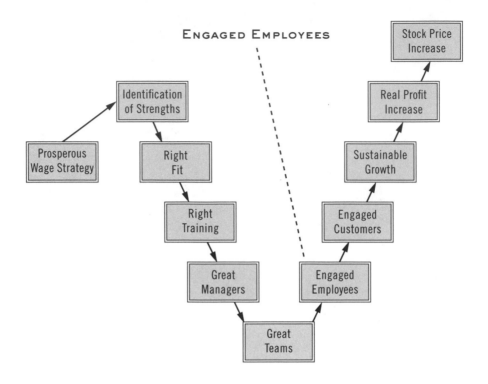

"Eighteen years." Her voice carried a certain pride and factual satisfaction. We guessed later that she was in her late thirties. That would mean she had started working there in high school or shortly thereafter—and had spent probably almost half her life at this local restaurant. She added, "I'm one of the new ones," as she pointed to the other servers, rattling off each name and that person's length of service. Talk about celebrating continuity and tenure!

The restaurant business is notorious for turnover. Here, however, we dined in the midst of an anomaly, especially given that the average meal ticket is probably less than $10 a person. My lunch companion respectfully acknowledged her service, but probed a bit further: "Eighteen years for you! Wow, that's amazing! What's kept you here for so long?"

A huge smile crossed her face. "See these people?" She gave a wave of an open hand across the room, indicating her coworkers and customers both. "I love them. This is like family. I absolutely love coming to work here."

This one-minute exchange provided an authentic lesson on what it means to be part of a Great Team. Our gratuity reflected our appreciation for her great service and her advice about a Great Team environment and the power of an Engaged Employee. Somewhere in that restaurant is a Great Manager who has created a winning Great Team culture that meaningfully engages employees—to the great benefit of the customers. This is the power of a Great Manager who inspires employees to master their jobs.

As discussed in the previous chapter, weak leadership at the top in a business culture adversely affects people downstream on the job. When faced with managers like those found in the comic strip *Dilbert*, even the most conscientious associate will eventually throw up his or her hands in frustration, give up trying to make a difference, and just go with the flow. Feeling helpless to change attitudes and the course of events is a sure route to high turnover and reduced profits.

On the other hand, winning is infectious. It attracts and retains employees, builds customer loyalty, invites investors to commit, and creates vendors and suppliers who want to be a part of something special. People will apply their best services and ideas to the benefit of a winning company, because their standards are elevated and taking initiative is rewarded.

It's a company's culture that creates the right environment for this winning attitude among employees. The more clearly defined and communicated corporate culture is, the more engaged the employees will be—and the better the company will hold together and perform. Clarity of culture is powerful, provided it doesn't go too far and become legalistic or an end unto itself. And yet a corporate culture will both attract and repel candidates for employment. This book provides job candidates with in-depth insight into our workplace. Some will race with excitement at the possibility of working within our company;

others that don't subscribe to our culture will run for the hills. We're thankful for both results.

As chief executive officer, my title might very well be chief cultural officer; the CEO is the person who sets the corporate culture and direction of the company. Just as with a church, however, our business is the people—the employees—not the buildings, systems, and departments. Our company culture holds us together in ways that business models alone cannot. Marketing and advertising may make promises. It is the people inside the company, however, who ultimately deliver on those promises. Our customer experience is a direct extension of the health of our corporate and store culture.

By now, you've gathered that our top managers and I have a strategic perspective that holds both long-term investments *and* short accounts on operational productivity. These are mutually inclusive for us; each depends upon the other. Both views bring value, but they must be reconciled in the short run through right actions that compound into the future. This integration produces sustainable personal and business growth, resulting in extraordinary profits. In terms of the human psyche, it also just *feels* right. This means we are constantly working toward improvement both "upstream" and "downstream" on our river of corporate culture. This also proves that hiring for excellence in every role increases employee engagement and profitability every time.

MEASURING ENGAGEMENT WITH THE Q^{12} SURVEY

Because it trusts the theory that high employee engagement equates to better company profits, the Gallup Organization administers a survey called the Q^{12} to measure employee engagement. Gallup's website explains it as follows:

Research published by Gallup and others has shown that engaged employees are more productive. The research also proves that engaged employees are more profitable, more customer-focused, safer, and more likely to withstand temptations to leave. Many have long suspected the connection between an employee's level of engagement and the level and quality of his or her performance. Our research has laid the matter to rest.

Yes, Gallup's research has thoroughly laid the matter to rest. Considering that the body of research in 2008 was based on surveys of 5.16 million employees in 537,678 workgroups throughout 455 organizations across fifteen major industries in 124 countries and forty-five languages—the evidence is definitive. The organization has published its findings and recommendations in the book *12: The Elements of Great Managing*, by Rodd Wagner and James K. Harter, PhD.

Here, with Gallup's permission, are the preamble and twelve statements of the Q^{12} survey:

How satisfied are you with your place of employment as a place to work? Rate this 1 (low) to 5 (high).

1. I know what is expected of me at work.

2. I have the materials and equipment I need to do my work right.

3. At work, I have the opportunity to do what I do best every day.

4. In the last seven days, I have received recognition or praise for doing good work.

5. My supervisor, or someone at work, seems to care about me as a person.

6. There is someone at work who encourages my development.

7. At work, my opinions seem to count.

8. The mission or purpose of my organization makes me feel my job is important.

9. My associates or fellow employees are committed to doing quality work.

10. I have a best friend at work.

11. In the last six months, someone at work has talked to me about my progress.

12. This last year, I have had opportunities at work to learn and grow.

In reading these, are you struck by the nature of each statement? First, each is stated from an employee's point of view, in everyday language rather than "management speak." Second, the Q^{12} provides amazing insight into employees' needs and interests. Third, to rank high in each affirmation is a hard-won victory, achieved over time and with the development of relationships; this survey is not a matter of quick fixes or a handful of best practices. Fourth, each statement is an end, not a means. In other words, someone needed to proactively perform in order to satisfy the statement. Fifth, not one statement involves financial compensation. Finally, each statement focuses on what is civilized and humane about the participant's job, because the survey measures the way we should treat one another.

While the Q^{12} statements appear simple, there is actually tremendous power behind each one. They evoke a visceral response that reflects so much of what is working (or isn't) in a company culture. The twelve statements are all linked to at least one of the four expected business outcomes: productivity, profitability, retention, and customer satisfaction. According to the Gallup Organization, the Q^{12} has withstood rigorous tests over time and is applicable to *any* business unit.

Put plainly, the Q^{12} reflects the level of pollution in the corporate culture at the river's mouth. Study the mouth of the river and you can learn a lot about a company. These responses can't be faked or easily turned around by implementing a best practice or making a pronouncement. There's an enduring quality about each statement that is indicative of a relationship and of learning over time along the brooks and creeks that collect and contribute to the forming of culture. It isn't a measurement of best practices *in theory*, either. Any company that uses this survey must actively create and maintain right behaviors in order to produce right results. Gallup measures and recommends, but we have to execute along the way—from the source to the mouth—to get desired results.

WORKPLACE TEAMS AND PROFITABILITY

Managers, teams, and employees are inextricably intertwined. Gallup, however, unravels the ball of string and prescribes an initial focus on developing Great Managers, who will then build Great Teams that can then cultivate Engaged Employees. This sequence points to the importance of building a team culture greater than that of the individual performer. It is a *system* of star players, not merely a collection of star players.

Do we have Great Teams? Our survey results lay that question to rest. Gallup places us, yet again, in its "Best Practice" class category. The majority of our workplace teams fall into the "world-class" group, or the top quartile of Gallup's database of more than half a million workplace teams.

Great Teams are the result of Great Managers. Continuity and increasing productivity, more than any other measures, are the best predictors of success. Let's say two seasoned managers are each producing more than a half a million dollars in store profits each year. We switch the managers. We could expect that both stores might fall to first-year profit levels, or about half their prior-year productivity. Why? Because while each manager has all the same knowledge, they do not have the team relationships in their new store. Each is in a rebuilding mode. In time, these managers will very likely build both stores back to championship status again. But why start all over again? Changing out talented managers is a rare happening at our company. Now you know why: It is very expensive to lose momentum and performance.

As noted earlier, one finds the same phenomenon in college and professional sports. Great coaches tend to create momentum and a system that works to produce consistent results. High turnover of head coaches, on the other hand, tends to produce teams that don't win championships. There are exceptions from time to time, but often this is a case of the team's momentum carrying it forward for a brief period. A revolving door of managers almost always means a drop in performance.

Furthermore, a Great Manager can lose team members but not suffer great losses in productivity. With our Strategic Path in hand, these managers have a way of folding new people into their store operations and getting people productive. A Great Manager has built bench strength (SMART Move 29), which softens the impact of team member turnover. The proof is in our Store Manager Continuity Chart, highlighted earlier in the book (see page 38). Managers on the job two or more years in the same store post high profits year in and year out, despite projected turnover. True, a new team member brings a new dynamic to the team. The store's figures may dip for a month or two during assimilation, but profits tend to recover quickly.

ENGAGING TALENTED PEOPLE

Productivity growth is the prime engine of a sustainable cost advantage and the only source of sustainable compensation growth for employees. Hiring talented people for every job at every level embeds the potential for growth in productivity across the company. There are many kinds of talents. The right talents—more than experience, brainpower, or willpower—are the prerequisites for Engaged Employees to perform with excellence in every role. *We've discovered that talent cannot be learned.* Talent is an inherent trait upon which growth can be fostered through Right Training. Strengths and talent, working in unison with Right Fit, are a high predictor of employee engagement and productivity.

In addition to the numerical data, Gallup's annual survey of our team members captured the following statements:

> "Recognition makes this company different."
>
> "I would lie in front of a bus for my region leader."
>
> "Other companies don't have our culture."
>
> "This company changed my life."
>
> "My job is to help us grow."

Employee engagement is alive and well, and improving steadily. Since we first began working with Gallup in 2003, we've seen a steady increase in our already high percentage of employee engagement, along with a decrease in disengaged employees as we've rooted out the brotherhood of the miserable (SMART Move 17).

SMART MOVE 34
Give employees an informal Q^{12} survey.
Review the Q^{12} questions with your team members to gain insight into employees' needs and interests. Measuring employee engagement can reveal links to greater profitability.

The Q^{12} survey provides amazing insight into employees' needs and interests. Each question is an end, not a means; rather than identifying best practices or giving abstract feedback, it actively measures the value of your company culture. The survey tells you if your team members are happy with the way they feel they have been treated.

Each Q^{12} statement evokes an insightful response that can reveal what works at the company. The twelve statements on the Q^{12} are all linked to at least one of four expected business outcomes: productivity, profitability, retention, and customer satisfaction. By asking employees to rate their satisfaction alongside each of these statements, you can pinpoint engagement, putting you ahead of the curve on improving profitability.

SMART MOVE 35
Once you know what's broken, fix it!
Education is not just about learning; it is about action. The Q^{12} tells you what is important and needs improvement. When scores are low, fix the problem!

During its many years of polling, Gallup has learned the right questions to ask. By reviewing employees' responses to the Q^{12} questions, you will find out if you are providing your team members with the following four attributes: basic needs, leadership support, teamwork, and growth. The figure on the following page sums up these four areas by stating the internal questions employees may ask themselves about their work.

In questions 1 and 2, if the answers to these questions score low, you need to focus on meeting your team members' needs. Questions 3 through 6 refer to the kind of leadership they are receiving. The responses to questions 7 through 10 tell you whether you are providing a team environment and whether everyone feels they are part of the team. Questions 11 and 12 will give you answers about whether your team members feel they have been given the opportunity to learn and grow.

QUESTION PYRAMID

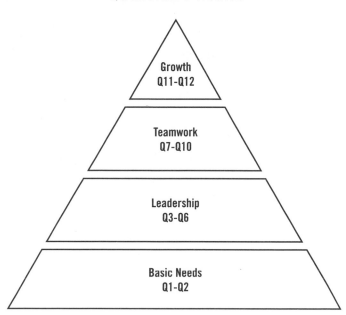

Growth
Q11-Q12

Teamwork
Q7-Q10

Leadership
Q3-Q6

Basic Needs
Q1-Q2

SMART MOVE 36
Develop a path toward leadership behavior.

The Q^{12} questions are about great leadership. You have to ask the right questions to find out what people really think. Use the responses you get on your Q^{12} survey as a tool to guide managers in achieving leadership behavior.

After surveys are completed by the Gallup Organization, the results are reported back to every level of management. Each management team member is given Q^{12} data that represents the overall outcome of the survey. The scores reflect what actions need to take place to improve results. Each team member is required to create an action plan and report to his or her immediate supervisor as it is carried out. These plans are monitored, and improved scores are expected on the next survey.

CHAPTER SUMMARY

KEY POINTS

- Corporate culture will both attract and repel potential employees. Because our culture is well defined, candidates are either readily a fit or clearly not a fit. As a result, the ones who remain with us tend to be highly engaged.

- The Gallup Q^{12} survey is the third-party assessment tool that we use to measure employee engagement. This assures an independent and objective assessment of our culture and of future profits.

- Our ratio of actively disengaged to engaged employees puts us in Gallup's "World Class" category, or top one-tenth of a percentile.

SMART MOVE 34

Give employees an informal Q^{12} survey.

Review the Q^{12} questions with your team members to gain insight into employees' needs and interests. Measuring employee engagement can reveal links to greater profitability.

SMART MOVE 35

Once you know what's broken, fix it!

Education is not just about learning; it is about action! The Q^{12} tells you what is important and needs improvement. When scores are low, find the problem and fix it!

SMART MOVE 36

Develop a path toward leadership behavior.

The Q^{12} questions are about great leadership. You have to ask the right questions to find out what people really think. Use the responses you get on your Q^{12} survey as a tool to guide managers in achieving leadership behavior.

CHAPTER 9

ENGAGED CUSTOMERS: *HOW DO YOU ACQUIRE SUCH LOYAL, PROFITABLE CUSTOMERS?*

The aim of marketing is to know and understand the customer so well that the product or service fits him and sells itself.

Peter Drucker, *The Essential Drucker*

THE PAWN INDUSTRY GENERALLY CATERS TO TWO GROUPS OF CUSTOMERS: PEOPLE WHO WANT TO BORROW MONEY AGAINST COLLATERAL AND BARGAIN SHOPPERS FROM ALL SOCIOECONOMIC LEVELS. As in any business, the Right Customers (like the Right Fit employees) are predictable, loyal, and profitable. Consistently engaging the Right Customers is the key to ongoing company profitability and the many benefits of mutual loyalty.

Absent a strategy and method like our Strategic Path to cultivate and produce enthusiastic fans, Engaged Customers are more happenstance.

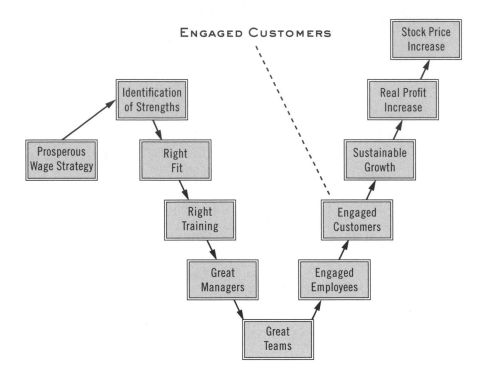

For great customer experiences to be a daily occurrence, they must originate "upstream," within the company culture and business model. Our history and experience has worn a path—our Strategic Path—so we can more predictably and consistently deliver world-class results.

THE REGULARS PHENOMENON

In the restaurant and bar business, there's a group of people known as "the regulars." These are the people who, for example, show up every Friday night at about the same time and, to a person, order just about the same meal and drinks. The manager, the waitstaff, and the regulars often know one another by name and certainly by sight. The waitress walks up to the table and asks, "The usual?"

Through conversation, they discover how life is treating one another. To the casual observer, it is small talk, right? Far from it. The accumulation of "small talk" over time is a big deal in the human experience. It is the groundwork of friendship and community building that leads to loyalty and trust.

Regulars bring friends to their favorite place. They recommend and refer thereby improving the business. Everyone is still doing business, but you're in each other's lives supportively; some would even say you're actually friends.

"The regulars" phenomenon can be true of any business, but is especially prevalent in retail service businesses like ours. Where there is ongoing customer contact, there is the potential for the benefits offered by regulars. The reason is simple: Both the customer and the business have selected each other as favorites.

Our Strategic Path has allowed us to be very intentional about gaining the benefits of "the regulars" phenomenon. Regulars aren't a matter of happenstance; we're built by design for them. By now, you know the story: High employee and management tenure plus continuity in the same location make a difference to the Right Customers. Regulars can't become engaged if everything and everyone keeps changing. Stability, order, and consistency of team members attract regulars. Regardless of whether it's a pizza or sub shop franchise or a high-end steak house like Ruth's Chris, the regulars are the Right Customers. This setup is good for people, it's good marketing, and it's great for the business.

Relationships of many kinds build, and a customer history develops. Our sales associates look out for things we know our customers are interested in buying or selling, and we call them. These customers have a friend in the business—something almost everyone appreciates, especially regulars.

THE RIGHT CUSTOMER

The customer is always right is a well-known saying in many circles of business—but we're decidedly focused on the "Right Customers." Every customer is treated respectfully, but the regulars naturally get that extra personal touch. The Right Customers have the potential to become predictable, loyal, and profitable regulars. We've built the company to attract and retain this type of customer.

For the average middle- or upper-income person, the day-to-day world of our business is typically neither familiar nor what might be expected. A pawnshop is a different kind of retail experience. The energy and effort we invest in regulars may appear irrational without this tidbit of understanding: their dollar volume may not be high, but their velocity—their rapid, predictable rate of return—surely is.

We think of our regulars in terms of the lifetime value of the customer plus potential referrals of friends, neighbors, and family members. By being fair and honest, and by thinking relationally over time, we're establishing the opportunity for a stream of profitable transactions for years, if not decades. A profitable relationship sets a different tone for transactions. Whereas a purely transactional person might be inclined to "go for the kill" and maximize profit, we're willing to earn a little less per transaction if it helps us gain a repeat customer.

Surprising to our new customers is the treatment they receive. The hallmark of our service is kindness, respect, dignity, and fairness. To borrow from the Ritz-Carlton hotel chain, "We are Ladies and Gentlemen serving Ladies and Gentlemen." Why not? Is the working class any less deserving? We have the privilege of serving people who generally aren't considered the privileged. Not only is our service honorable, it is meaningful, because we make a difference in the lives of our customers *every day*. That's personally and financially rewarding work.

Right Customers like seeing the same face serving them when they visit our stores. When they hear their name and are remembered, it makes for a positive experience. The relationship can pick up where it left off. By comparison, walking into a store filled with strangers might be acceptable, but it's not as friendly. To have "a friend in the business" creates a more enjoyable, safe, and rewarding way to conduct one's business. From the customer's point of view, being cared for by a friend beats dealing with a stranger any day. A new customer may begin as a complete stranger, but those who fit our Right Customer profile quickly convert into regulars.

Our goal is to treat every customer right. We explain every transaction up front. Retention and satisfaction with our customers gives us a tremendous competitive cost and market advantage. Frankly, these relationships boost employee spirits, feelings of belonging, and productivity. When you care for someone and their family, you want to do right by them.

ORGANIC GROWTH

Our stores typically serve a neighborhood within the surrounding two-mile radius. Our long-tenured managers watch babies become teens, support Little League teams, and provide community leadership. Saturdays are often special days designed, through a variety of promotions, to bring the neighbors together and drive store traffic. We like to make our shops happening places. On Black Friday, the day after Thanksgiving, we typically have people lined up in front of the door to get in early.

Great relationships are a vital contributor to a strong and profitable business. There's a mutual respect between the employees and the customers. Our customers learn the rules of the game and know we adhere to our way of doing business.

The culminating event of all our efforts at developing our business model and culture is a customer referral. When one customer tells another person about us and that person becomes a customer, then

organic business growth is happening. There's no better or more important indicator of sustainable growth and profits than an expanding base
of Right Customers.

RESULTS

Think we can talk a good game? Maybe so, but Gallup Consulting
customer surveys keep us honest. Gallup refers to Right Customers
as "Engaged Customers." Its independent third-party assessment takes
our perceptions and converts them into facts the CE[11] survey of our
customers. Like the Q[12] for employees, the CE[11] measures "customer
engagement": customers' attitudes and experiences. With Gallup's permission, here are the questions and statements used:

CE1.   Taking into account all the products and services
       you receive from them, how satisfied are you with
       the company overall?

CE2.   How likely are you to continue to use the company?

CE3.   How likely are you to recommend the company to
       a friend or associate?

CE4.   Our name is a name I can always trust.

CE5.   The company always delivers on its promises.

CE6.   The company always treats me fairly.

CE7.   If a problem arises, I can always count on the com-
       pany to reach a fair and satisfactory resolution.

CE8.   I feel proud to be a customer.

CE9.   The company always treats me with respect.

CE10. The company is perfect for people like me.

CE11. I can't imagine a world without the company.

Comparing us to Gallup's top 10 percent of companies, we equal or exceed the benchmark scores on every measure, year after year. Our results are considered "world-class" by Gallup Consulting, as they position us in the 92nd percentile in Gallup's global customer database. These benchmarks come from Gallup's database of three million customers spanning forty-eight thousand business units in 197 organizations scattered across sixteen industries in fifty-three countries. For us to earn these high marks, our customers have to strongly agree with a certain number of loyalty and engagement statements that Gallup consultants ask in their customer surveys. For example, more than 68 percent of our surveyed customers agree or strongly agree that they can't imagine a world without us, and 88 percent agree or strongly agree that we're the perfect company for them. The same percentage believes we treat them fairly. Gallup tells us that these results are significantly more positive than those for the vast majority of companies Gallup has consulted with over the years.

Let's put this another way. While Gallup doesn't release comparative individual company statistics, I firmly believe that within our industry we offer customer service and loyalty on par with or better than such world-class companies as The Ritz-Carlton Hotel Company, Wells Fargo Bank, Best Buy, Chick-fil-A, and Publix.

What makes our numbers so unbelievable for the person outside our target audience is an inability to relate to our particular environment. Our system runs counter to business models in which extraordinary customer service is typically reserved for the upper-income earners. Our way of doing business may seen unconventional, but it is the reason we are so successful by most any measure, for any type of business. Serving the Right Customers the right way perpetuates productivity and profitability.

SMART MOVE 37
Build the business for the Right Customer.

Not all customers are profitable, and our business can't be all things to all people. Instead, we need to find and acquire the right kind of customer—one who will provide steady cash flow and a profitable return on investment for years to come.

The customer is almost never wrong.

César Ritz

In the early 1900s, Cesar Ritz discovered the value of finding and serving the Right Customer and treating that customer well. Like Henry Ford, Ritz knew that for his hotel chain, certain customers were profitable while others were not.

When considering our Right Customer, we use three rules:

1. People like to do business with people they know and trust. This is true for customers and employees alike. Customers who have developed stable, long-term relationships with our managers and our store staff do more business with us. Our manager continuity statistics prove this rule.

2. Some customers are more profitable for us than others are. They pay service charges on time, and require less attention and service because we're mutually efficient in conducting transactions.

3. Kindness and fairness are free to give, and pay dividends in word-of-mouth business growth. Our world-class customer service and favorable policies attract people who want to be treated fairly and feel as though they have an inside track to the company.

The more customers we can attract who fit in one or more of the three groups above, the better our chances of reaping the rewards of high customer retention. In practice, these rewards tend to spiral upward, building on their own success. Better customers create a more profitable cash flow.

Research in Frederick Reichheld's book *The Loyalty Effect* states that customers who like long-term relationships tend to "lock in" with a vendor. They are the hardest to persuade to switch from a competitor, even for a significant price savings. They place a high value on trust and reduced risk. Meanwhile, other people are price shoppers and will jump for even a 2 percent savings.

In the final analysis, the only way to attract and retain Right Customers is to provide outstanding customer service consistent with the Right Customers' expectations. What makes it confusing for many businesspeople is the simple question, who is my Right Customer? Trial and error is one way to eventually discover your Right Customer—an expensive and dangerous way. The other way is to think forwardly and strategically about what one is attempting to build, via strategy, tactics, and results. There will still be plenty of trial and error, but the learning will have a basis against which to measure. Our Strategic Path provides that platform for learning and improvement.

SMART MOVE 38
Do not outsource customer service.
Bring customer service as close to the customer as you can. Do not outsource it! This will build customer loyalty and trust in your business.

We offer total service to our customers by having a jeweler available in every store. This surprises people both inside and outside of our industry, but jewelry is a big percentage of our business and we're serious about it. An on-site jeweler provides the customer with immediate service. We can also help with repairs and cleaning, often for no charge. Jewelers are a great investment because everyone wins: The customers get the convenience of one-stop shopping, so they continue to bring us their business.

Jewelry retail chains typically centralize their jewelers rather than staffing one at each location, ostensibly to gain operational efficiency and personnel savings. Having a jeweler readily available, however, brings an amazing return on investment. By the time our competitors handle, pack, insure, ship, assess, track, and return jewelry, we've already sold the item. Our time to market is hours, not days or weeks. Our lower inventory carrying costs further justify the investment, and we also avoid the opportunity cost of lost sales and profits.

Jewelers are constantly cleaning and repairing our merchandise, so it looks like new when displayed. Jewelers make sure all the parts are working and in order. Should a problem arise, our jeweler is there to fix it. Our trusted reputation for jewelry exists because our customers are confident that the product value is fair.

A jeweler means convenience. For example, a ring often can be sized immediately. A one-stop shop saves our customers time and effort. Giving gifts is even more satisfying when the ring fits the finger correctly.

Apply this to any business: Do the customer service at the store! You'll neither save money nor increase profits by outsourcing customer service.

CHAPTER SUMMARY

KEY POINTS

- Our Strategic Path creates a momentum or flow that leads to the customer experience. A defined culture creates a customer experience that tends to engage customers. We're not the store for everybody, but the people we serve love us.

- All customers are not profitable! We cannot serve unprofitable customers.

- Many of our customers are "regulars"—people with whom we have a trusted, long-standing relationship.

- We use Gallup Consulting's CE[11] survey to assess customer engagement. We are in Gallup's "World Class" category.

SMART MOVE 37
Build the business for the Right Customer.

Not all customers are profitable, and our business can't be all things to all people. Instead, we need to find and acquire the right kind of customer—one who will provide steady cash flow and a profitable return on investment for years to come.

SMART MOVE 38
Do not outsource customer service.

Bring customer service as close to the customer as you can. Do not outsource it! This will build customer loyalty and trust in your business.

CHAPTER 10

SUSTAINABLE GROWTH: AT WHAT POINT DO YOUR STORES' REVENUES PEAK?

Give a man a fish, and you feed him for a day.
Teach him how to fish, and you feed him for a lifetime.

FREQUENTLY, I'M QUESTIONED ABOUT THE MAXIMUM PROFIT POTEN-TIAL OF OUR STORES. This misses the mark, because it is asking me to place limits on people's talent and smarts. No way! Who am I to place such limits? Why would I ever want to answer that question and cap our potential? We're into team members setting new records, achieving the unachievable, and producing unimagined real profits. We're a company of cheerleaders, and I'm the biggest one. We root for our people to discover new and better ways to do business. They can then share with the rest of us how they accomplished the "impossible." We can celebrate them and blend into our practices what they've learned, to help us all improve.

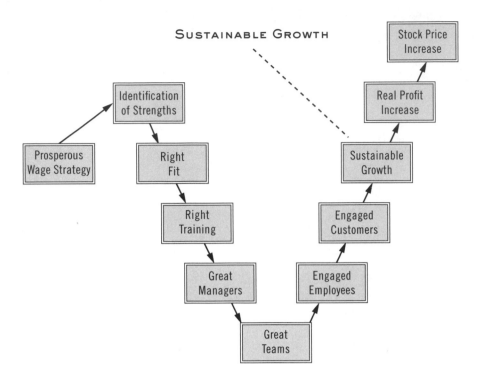

SUSTAINABLE GROWTH

Sustainable Growth means the business never peaks. Regardless of whether "the business" is defined as one person, one store, one region, or an entire company, the defining question is always, are we capable of better? The answer isn't a matter of operations, marketing, finances, or human resources systems; it isn't dependent upon market conditions, the economy, or world affairs. The answer to this question comes down to one thing: belief in being better.

Being better begins as a personal choice that we want every team member to make, both personally and professionally. Sustainable Growth in the business is not possible until every person on the team believes improvement is possible. Our business relies on the collective confidence of our team. In light of this, our Strategic Path helps our people more fully realize the potential team contribution each of them can make. The company is the beneficiary of this upward curve in competence and confidence.

Simply stated, stores or functioning entities will not peak when management focuses on reducing employee turnover, increasing continuity among staff, and consistently reviewing individual productivity. While this is not a secret formula for success, it's been proven to work at our company. Sustainable Growth, therefore, is heavily dependent on the ability of management to focus on the right things.

NUTRIENTS

There are no shortcuts to Sustainable Growth. It requires a mind-set and philosophy of doing business that must be taught and learned throughout the organization. The word *sustain* is derived from the combination of two Latin words: *sus-* ("up") and *tenere* ("to hold"). The taproot for growth here is our Strategic Path, and the lateral roots are the SMART Moves; these support the upward growth of the company. It has taken years of learning to develop our Strategic Path and to discern which moves aren't so smart and which are SMART Moves.

Jim Collins and Jerry Porras's book *Built to Last* explains how to lay a foundation for building a company for the long haul rather than the quick hit. The authors emphasize the importance of long-term thinking that influences short-term actions. By comparison, many a businessperson's driving thought is only short-term: *What can make me the most money right now?* Then he or she acts based on this assessment. In fact, this approach often produces only immediate income, which appears to be justifiable but soon fizzles out. Because of the apparent reward, however, this behavior becomes a pattern of quick profit-taking hits. There is often a "feast or famine" lifestyle associated with this approach. Many salespeople or small businesspeople find themselves in this ultimately depleting work cycle. In contrast, the long-term business builder invests appropriate time in the business to develop systems that create sustainable advantages and profit-making opportunities.

We do many things right, providing the proper "nutrients" to sustain the company's potential growth, yet we haven't even scratched the surface of what's possible. Every day in every role we're getting better and better from within.

TRAINING AND SUSTAINING

Training falls into two broad categories: skills and knowledge. Most training is focused on giving people the knowledge necessary to learn and comply with job expectations and standards. Knowledge training, however, is about transforming a person's thinking, perspective, values, and ultimately, decision-making ability. We invest heavily in knowledge training because this is how people become successful.

Competence leads to confidence. Our Strategic Path is primarily concepts-based training integrated with skills-based training to create a more comprehensive learning experience. Even confident people, when faced with a new challenge, are apt to be less than bold. There's a learning curve involved. Our Strategic Path and our culture of learning uphold all of our team members, allowing them to grow in competence and, therefore, in confidence.

This may all sound good to you, but are you wondering why it matters to the business? Here's why: Competent and confident people tend to be more engaged in their life and work. They bring a positive "can do" attitude to those around them. Confident people are more apt to explore beyond their comfort zone into growth areas. This risk-taking attitude births new ideas and innovations that make the business better. When every productive team member is also constantly working to innovate and improve, then the business is apt to thrive. There is no peak to performance when competent, confident people are involved.

Sustainable Growth is an attitude of the heart and mind before it is ever a result in the pocketbook. I can unequivocally state that within our industry, we have the world's best personal and professional development program, and that leads our team members into an abundance of spirit, friendships, and finances.

Our advantages in the market come down to one thing: We value our people. Our team members get better every day, and so the company continues to grow in revenues and profits. Yes, we're adding stores through *de novo* development and select mergers and acquisitions, but none of this is possible without people who are growing both on and off the job.

A growing company is different than a company that experiences Sustainable Growth. Both types of companies share a profit motive and are typically measured by similar Wall Street benchmarks or other analytics. But for the company that is only growing, the concepts of sustainability and momentum aren't in the box scores, so they're often overlooked. *Sustainable* implies that the business has depth and can renew as necessary to continue growth. *Momentum* speaks to the weight and inclination of the organization to move forward.

As a Sustainable Growth company, we're organized by a different set of principles, perspectives, and measures than a growth company. We're built for the long haul, not the quick sale. We resist the temptation of many growth companies to manipulate the numbers in order to post and meet projections via rapid expansions or acquisitions that risk the corporate culture and stress operations. Paper profits may pump up the numbers that make the analysts swoon, but these maneuvers can often endanger the core business. Instead, we're focused on having the best team members with the greatest opportunity, who execute the fundamentals of our business with excellence. Profits are far more predictable in a company committed to Sustainable Growth.

SMART MOVE 39
Do not move people around.

Our continuity reports prove that moving people from location to location negatively affects every line item on the income statement. Sustained earnings growth occurs in stores where people have not been moved.

Many businesses move their people around, whether from department to department, store to store, or region to region. I am sure the reasons for some of these moves are good. However, I bet the majority of these moves happen because of staffing issues and a lack of bench strength. Our continuity report (below) is proof of sustained earnings growth in stores where people have not been relocated. If the income is double that of stores where personnel are rearranged, why would you move people around?

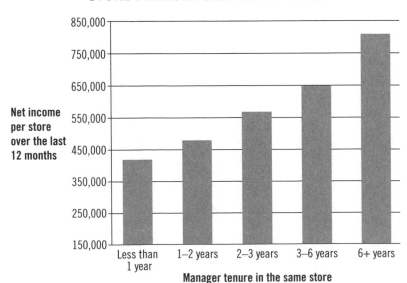

STORE MANAGER CONTINUITY CHART

CHAPTER SUMMARY

KEY POINTS

- Do store revenues ever peak? Not if management will focus on low employee turnover, increasing continuity among staff, and consistently reviewing individual productivity. There is no benefit to placing limits on people's imagination and talent. The right people in the right position, operating within their strengths with a great team, can achieve the "impossible": infinite growth.

- Sustainable growth is a long-term mind-set. It involves building a foundation or platform for growth based on principles and attitudes of lasting over time.

- The core of our Sustainable Growth is the belief that the company is doing well plus the confidence that we can get better every day.

SMART MOVE 39
Do not move people around.

Our continuity reports prove that moving people from location to location negatively affects every line item on the income statement. Sustained earnings growth occurs in stores where people have not been moved.

CHAPTER 11

REAL PROFIT INCREASE: AREN'T ALL PROFITS REAL?

Profits, like sausages . . . are esteemed most by those who know least about what goes into them.

Alvin Toffler, *Future Shock*

ALL PROFITS ARE REPORTED IN THE SAME WAY ON THE INCOME STATE-MENT, BUT NOT ALL PROFITS ARE THE SAME. There are "real profits" from operations—the sustainable result of operational excellence. Then there are "cosmetic profits" extracted from a business by excessive financial engineering; these maneuvers threaten the very existence of the organization. In Texas, this profit-taking approach is referred to as "eating your seed corn"—devouring the reserve of best seeds that a farmer intends to carry over from one growing season to the next, to ensure that he has corn to plant in the future.

Real profits, on the other hand, are harvested when you plant those excellent seeds each year. Prosperity and Real Profit Increase are

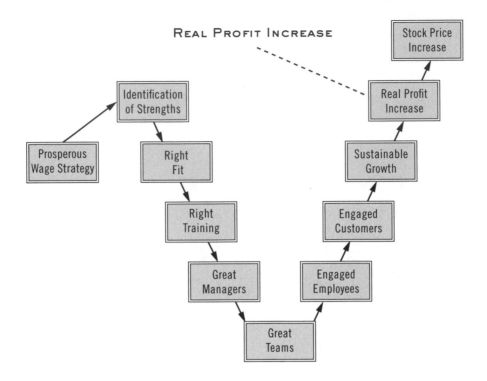

directly related. This clear, documented link is a blueprint for improving the fundamental contribution of our business to our employees, our customers, and our investors. Our Strategic Path provides both a design and a method of Real Profit Increase, where the whole is greater than the sum of the parts. The meaningful integration of people, operations, economics, and accounting into greater collective service is a hard-won standard of productivity. Real Profit Increase is a wholesome method that produces abundance for all the groups in the Triangle.

Our early shareholders developed a vision of building this business according to enduring standards, and for this I'm sincerely thankful. We've avoided short-sighted profit taking and instead invested in people, tapping into their desire to make a stable, long-term contribution to the world around them. Even before we knew about The Gallup Path, we were investing in the long-term well-being of employees and viewing them as the essential contributors to real retail profits, not a line item on the income statement. We know how to make a real profit: by investing in our team members.

PROFIT MAKING AND PROFIT TAKING

For simplicity's sake, let's say there are two types of profit: real and cosmetic. Real profit comes from operational excellence; it involves improving the core capacity of the business to operate more effectively and efficiently. Real Profit Increase is profit making within the fundamentals of the business. Our Strategic Path keeps our focus on real profits.

Cosmetic profit, however, is a result of financial engineering, and it derives from anything other than core business operations. These bottom-line numbers may reflect extraordinary events, exchange rate fluctuations, and accounting standard elections (examples of legitimate profit taking due to special circumstances or opportunity). They affect profit reporting but don't directly influence the fundamentals of the income statement above the gross margin.

The Gallup Consulting website's description of The Gallup Path adds perspective on the difference between real and cosmetic profits:

> Real profit increase can only be driven by sustainable growth. Sustainable growth is quite different from "bought growth." A company can buy growth through a variety of techniques: acquiring another company's earnings stream, slashing prices, or, a perennial favorite among fast-growing restaurant or retail chains, opening as many new locations as possible, as quickly as possible. All of these techniques create a welcome spike in your earnings, but none of them addresses the issue of sustaining those earnings—in fact, some of them actively undermine it. Sustainable growth is not measured by a short-lived earnings spike. Rather, sustainable growth

is measured by metrics such as earnings per store, or revenue per product, or number of services used per customer. These metrics reveal whether or not your revenue stream is robust, whether it will last.

Profit takers slash expenses with actions like across-the-board layoffs or indiscriminant expense cuts, to produce flashes of profit. They're making their budget, but killing the Golden Goose. This erosion of the core business relegates it to being in a state of constant crisis. Management by adrenaline may produce earning spikes, but it is typically accompanied by high turnover and lack of continuity due to burnout and disgust. It always leads to an unhealthy culture and underperforming results.

Our society seems to be breeding this "now mentality." Many of our new hires have to unlearn what they've experienced on prior jobs. There is nothing pretty about financially engineering earnings. Sadly, strategy, policies, compensation systems, and pressure to report good news often conspire to corrupt an organization's corporate culture. In these cases, the responsible party is more interested in *showing* a profit than in *making* a profit. A day of reckoning will come. Real profits, on the other hand, can't be massaged into being through clever expense cuts and sleight-of-hand accounting.

MANAGING TO A REAL PROFIT

Profit makers stand in sharp contrast to profit fakers and profit takers. Profit makers manage a business to a Real Profit Increase by, as Peter Drucker encouraged, "doing the right thing and doing things right." Real profit comes from deep within a business's strategy, culture, markets, and operations. Managers prepare team members to perform and then allow the results (profit) to inform the next "plan–do–review" season of improvement. Profit (or loss) is feedback, not the end game. Profit momentum and improvement provide context and continuity.

Real profit is the leading indicator of how well integrated and high performing the business is. Instead of playing games with the business, profit makers are playing the game of business with excellence.

Our Strategic Path and our SMART Moves compose a highly developed guidebook that allows individual performers and managers to be appropriately motivated, trained, and held accountable for social, economic, and financial results. These tools are highly predictive of a Real Profit Increase. By playing within the rules of the game, we repeatedly see bona fide results.

THE CAUSE OF PROFITS

Cause and effect are dear friends to those who manage a business to make a profit. In fact, our Strategic Path is an avenue to productivity that integrates the many perspectives on profits. It allows us to achieve world-class results for those in the SMART Moves Triangle while maintaining high standards and expectations across the company. Real Profit Increase is the organic product of improving the core strategic and operational realities of the business model and culture. Everything you've read thus far in this book contributes to creating a better employee and customer experience—resulting in a Real Profit Increase for investors and team members.

Profit takers instantly react adversely to our Strategic Path. They gag on the first step—a Prosperous Wage Strategy. They've built their business on paying people as little as possible rather than as much as they can, so they get what they pay for and deserve. "Overpaying" people goes

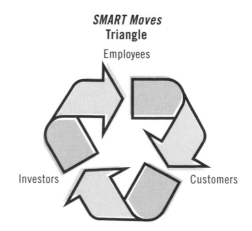

**SMART Moves
Triangle**

Employees

Investors

Customers

against their business psyche. Instead, they'll pay low wages and "let the cream rise to the top" of an ill-defined and subjective career path. They'll play with sales commissions, because salespeople are making "too much" money. As Henry Ford explained, low wages will kill a business, long before it kills the employee. And profit takers wonder why they have turnover, why they can't find any good people—why their business isn't making more money! Our Strategic Path is counterintuitive to profit takers, especially those who've fooled themselves into believing they are actually profit makers. Profit breeds profit; you can't cause profits in one area by withholding them in another.

A company of profit makers, on the other hand, feeds current needs and provides for the future. Succession planning is essential. When unhealthy turnover (SMART Move 2) happens in our company, the bench strength (SMART Move 29) exists for another profit maker to assume the position.

There are people who will cut down an apple tree in order to get the apples they want now. Nothing is left for those who would come behind them, as there will be no crop next year. Many a manager mistakenly manages profits instead of managing *to* a profit. Those seeking financial engineering have a shallow and skewed perspective of business. Those who manage to a profit see beyond the numbers and into the heads, hearts, and souls of the people—employees, customers, investors and the public—to organize the business in such a way that everyone benefits from the resulting profits. A business is more than an engine of economic means. It is a part of the social fabric of the country.

Any economics book will tell you that a business exists to make a profit. Read a sociology book and it will say that a business exists to improve society. Study an accounting book and you'll learn that profit is the remainder from revenue minus expenses. Which is the right take on it? The answer is that each is right within its discipline. These three views of a business are different, but not mutually exclusive.

SMART MOVE 40
Know what you mean by profit.
The economist sees profit as the essential outcome of a business that sustains it and allows it to thrive. The sociologist sees the organization in human terms and looks toward its contribution to making the world a better place. The accountant reports on a mathematical relationship. We've reconciled all three perspectives into a single, cohesive meaning and fulfillment of profit.

The businessman's challenge is to successfully integrate many disciplines to produce a real profit at the end of the period by all measures—economic, social, and accounting. Profit is vitally important, but it is a scorecard measure of a business's effectiveness, not a management method. For the press and politicians, "excessive profits" is a convenient sound bite. Healthy profit making, however, is the engine of progress and prosperity.

I am an evangelist for business. I'm also a realist, however: There are bad people out there doing business at the expense of everyone, with only their self-interest in mind. They may rise, but to sustain the business, they'll have to provide greater value than the cost of their goods or services. Otherwise, the free enterprise system will put them out of business.

Let's not focus on the exceptions. Instead, let's raise the bar of doing right in business. Real profits emerge from a conscious decision to treat people properly, constantly deliver and improve one's goods and services, and earn a profit worthy of one's contribution to the condition of mankind. Here is the nobility inherent in business that for too many people is never realized, nor experienced. We are all capable of being better.

It seems a simple enough concept: Responsibility for profits begins with the sales associates, continues through the store managers, and extends all the way through the organizational chart to my job as

SMART MOVE 41

Make profits possible.

Allow people to win honestly in service to others. Profit and loss responsibility must run throughout the company in order to make profits possible for everyone in the Triangle.

chairman and CEO. When our sales associates are making profits for themselves, then the company is profiting. Too many compensation systems are designed as financial controls rather than as liberators of the entrepreneurial spirit. Why do so many companies design their compensation systems so their people invariably lose?

Profit takers are myopically tied to short-term results, even at the risk of the long-term sustainability of the business. This practice is called "window dressing," which refers to the artificial pumping up of performance measures to give a better impression than the reality of the underlying performance. Window dressing is most often attributed to investment portfolio managers who manipulate their holdings just before the end of a reporting period in order to meet benchmark objectives. It is a deceptive yet legal practice by a person wanting to either look good or earn a bonus or both. The system rewards their deception, and that's just wrong.

Window dressing isn't limited to portfolio managers. It is an everyday practice done by anyone, but not everyone, who is responsible for the profit and loss of an entity—a sales territory, a department, or a company. Playing games with profit is not only a deceptive act but also a desperate act by people who are unable to get the job done otherwise. They're getting beaten, so they're cutting corners and hiding this fact in hopes that matters will eventually turn in their favor. Robbing Peter to pay Paul is still robbery, though. It isn't that they're necessarily bad people. Chances are they have never been led into true prosperity by a mentor. They're scraping by, doing the best they can with what knowledge and understanding they have. The ability to make money is a skill that can be learned, provided one has a qualified teacher. Suffice it to say, traditional education in this context can be nearly irrelevant.

The opposite of window dressing is "sandbagging," where the manager deceptively holds back information or profits in order to underreport profits. That may seem an odd practice to the casual observer unless you link it with motivation. Let's say a salesperson is 200 units short of his monthly quota and is going to miss earning his monthly bonus. On the last day of the month, he sells 185 units—close to his quota, but just shy of earning the bonus. He sandbags the order so he can get a head start in the new month with 185 units. His chances of earning a bonus in the new month have increased. This sleight of hand is so common that many salespeople aren't even aware that it is a dishonest practice in the eyes of their employer.

In any business our size, it would be easy to artificially pump up the numbers in order to post a profit to show our shareholders. This act is contrary to how we operate. It sets in motion an unhealthy addiction to *reporting* profits rather than a pursuit of operational excellence that *produces* profits. At that point, the business becomes a game of accounting instead of an engine of economic profit and social contribution. Here is where my character as the CEO matters the most. The temptation to please shareholders in the short term forces many of my CEO colleagues into a downward spiral; eventually, the house of cards comes crashing down around them. By training our entire company to follow our Strategic Path, we've developed a company of accountability partners. This keeps us all on the straight and true.

CHAPTER SUMMARY

KEY POINTS

- Not all profits are the same. Some profits are the predictable results of operational excellence. Other profits may be situational, due to some swing in the market for a good or service. Increasing operating profits is the primary fiscal responsibility of management and team members.

- Developing the mind-set of being a profit maker is a very different approach to doing business from that of a profit taker. Financial engineering is generally a short-term play, whereas profit making is the creation of systematically predictable profit. Single-minded profit maximization ultimately undermines sustainable profit-making capacity.

- We have been successful with cultivating a company of profit makers. While we excel at this, there is always room for improvement.

SMART MOVE 40
Know what you mean by profit.

The economist sees profit as the essential outcome of a business that sustains it and allows it to thrive. The sociologist sees the organization in human terms and looks toward its contribution to making the world a better place. The accountant reports on a mathematical relationship. We've reconciled all three perspectives into a cohesive meaning and fulfillment of profit.

SMART MOVE 41
Make profits possible.

Allow people to win honestly in service to others. Profit and loss responsibility must runs throughout the company in order to make profits possible for everyone in the Triangle.

CHAPTER 12

STOCK PRICE INCREASE: HOW DO YOU MEASURE THE HEALTH OF THE COMPANY?

Most people get interested in stocks when everyone else is. The time to get interested is when no one else is. In my business, you can't buy what is popular and do well.

Warren Buffett, CEO, Berkshire Hathaway

A STOCK PRICE INCREASE IS THE RESULT OF A RISE (OR A PERCEIVED RISE) IN THE UNDERLYING VALUE OF THE COMPANY. A Real Profit Increase precedes a Stock Price Increase and that may appear to be the endpoint of our Strategic Path: the investors earning an appreciation of their investment. In fact, a Stock Price Increase is just a beginning. Financial health means the company is positioned to reinvest in the employees and the business model.

Earlier in this book, our discussion about the SMART Moves Triangle pointed out that employees and investors both benefit

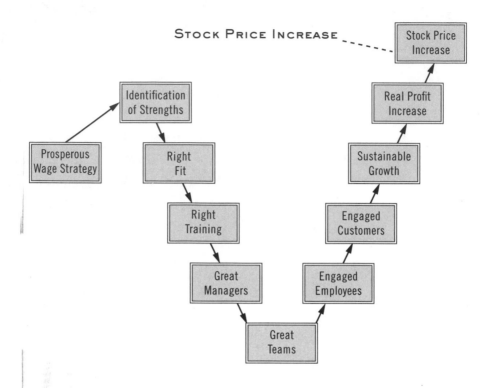

from good financial health. Higher wages can be paid for increased productivity. Greater resources can be earmarked for expansion. Stock prices can continue to see stability and growth. Investors who subscribe to the vision of the SMART Moves Triangle (see page 173) are apt to be patient, stable, and content with long-term appreciation. This is a win-win situation that allows for a stable financial position while providing a clear path for growth.

PEOPLE POWER PROFITS

In a "serving corporation," as Henry Ford describes it, people come first. This is the only way a company can fully realize its profit potential. If the people aren't first, then profit potential is hindered. Managing a company by its current stock price is a recipe for disaster. It is like a head football coach being on the sidelines and watching only the scoreboard. You can't lead a team to victory that way. The field of play must be observed and guided so the team can put points on the board. People are the source of true winning, so we pay close attention to having the very best personnel.

Stock Price Increase is typically an investor's measure of value because the shareholders are the obvious beneficiaries. In fact, stock price is also an indirect measure of the company's collective efforts as understood by the public (in the case of a publicly traded company).

Sustainable Growth and Real Profit Increase are the predecessors to a Stock Price Increase. When people and profits are growing, it is a winning and secure combination. Our dashboard isn't one-dimensional, limited to financial statements and ratios. Instead, our gauges include employee and customer engagement as surveyed by Gallup Consulting. The priority we place on these people measures sets us apart. Gallup's services have enabled us to refine and define standards on the otherwise mysterious side of business: managing people and serving customers.

Gallup's audit of our team members is as important a management tool as the financial audit performed by our CPAs. The state of our people is the best indicator of our business health, our prosperity, and ultimately, our financial potential. Measuring engagement provides feedback and insights that help to focus our organization so we can achieve world-class standing. Before Gallup, we knew our people skills were strong, but we could not measure our employee and customer engagement statistics; now we can deal with facts, not opinions. Gallup has provided clear and powerful tools, measures, and insights so we quantifiably know how well we're doing as a company and compared to the world's best companies. Stock Price Increase is an important result and a measure of a company's success, but it's essential to remember what truly powers such profit: the people behind any organization.

FUNDAMENTALS AND FASHION

While private companies focus on sound business practices to generate profits, publicly traded companies and their stock prices are more a function of fundamentals and fashion. Market sectors, industries, and companies come in and out of favor with Wall Street for sound, tangible reasons as well as purely psychological reasons. Fluctuating market moods impact a company's stock price, but are mostly beyond the control of the company. Stock price is constantly assessed by investors, and so it may be difficult for management to communicate real value. To a degree, however, perceptions can be managed through communications, public relations, marketing, and investor relations.

Regardless of whether a company is private or public, let's strip away the perceptions and fashion of the stock markets and drill down to the financial foundation. In this regard, the stock price measure that tells the most unvarnished story of a business is the book value per share. This internal stock price, if you will, strips out market perceptions and preferences, and deals with the pure numbers. Even then, one must be cautious to segment Real Profit Increase in the owner's equity from cosmetic or extraordinary profit. Given this caveat, if the book value stock price is increasing, then the market stock price, in theory, should rise. The market stock price and the book value price are not always in sync, due to differing investor valuations and needs, but in general they are aligned.

Operationally, we have a business mind-set of cash-on-cash return. We are focused on the basics of profit making per store. This simple and straightforward measure keeps our attention manageable. In good conscience, the fundamentals must be the first order of business if our book value is to increase. Our second order of business, then, is to present ourselves accurately and smartly so investors appreciate who we are, where we are headed, how we intend to get there, and what we value as important to winning. We want to be a company of both steak and sizzle, not just the sizzle with no real meat to it.

In light of this, our Strategic Path provides a commitment for our employees and our investors alike—a basic blueprint for success. We expect to be held accountable to this plan to achieve Stock Price Increase; that is how we ensure that our business is sound and the parties within our Triangle reap the benefits. Our Strategic Path orders and integrates the underlying causes of profit making rather than falling prey to the more obvious but potentially undermining maneuvers of profit taking. Very simply put, our company engages the right employees caring for the Right Customers. This provides our investors and the public with a world-class contribution of profits and service, respectively.

CHAPTER SUMMARY

KEY POINTS

- Stock price is a function of both real and perceived value. In private companies, the real value of the business generated from net operating profits, and sound business management is the focus. In public companies, where the stock price is being assessed moment to moment by investors with motivation and incentives often different than those of the company, the importance of communicating real value brings an added level of responsibility to management.

- Our Strategic Path allows us to increase real profits consistently. Perceptions are challenging to manage, even among our private investors. Results, however, are always the best offense and defense for managing perceived value. This ensures that the stock price is more representative of value.

CHAPTER 13

THE VERY POINT OF LIFE: WHY DO YOU CARE SO MUCH ABOUT YOUR TEAM MEMBERS?

Enduring great companies don't exist merely to deliver returns to shareholders. Indeed, in a truly great company, profits and cash flow become the blood and water to a healthy body: They are absolutely essential for life, but they are not the very point of life.

Jim Collins, *Good to Great*

JIM COLLINS IS BOLD ENOUGH TO DIRECT OUR ATTENTION TO THE ESSENTIAL QUESTION, WHAT IS THE VERY POINT OF LIFE? and wise enough to tell us that profit and cash flow aren't it. He implies that there is something more, but stops short of telling us what that point might be. The answer, of course, varies from person to person.

One's perspective will have an impact on how that person deals with others. When a person genuinely values people, he or she brings optimism and respect to the table. This general sense of well-being translates into feelings of value, security, and trust. This, in turn, provides a great foundation for positive and productive teams.

Work matters to people. A positive and productive leader can align employee needs quickly into a productive team by simply understanding why the point of life is important to everyone. When you have hired with the "Excellence in every role" mantra, and your employees are up to speed, they are fully engaged and competent. The real benefit here? They will retain this approach for the course of their employment, and your company will be the best in the business.

MAKING A DIFFERENCE
WHILE MAKING A PROFIT

Too often, businesses hire those who are not best suited for the work that is to be done. The result is that many of these employees join the brotherhood of the miserable, and profitability suffers. Hiring for excellence in every role will help overcome this problem and allow employees to feel good about making a profit while serving customers in a positive and productive manner. There will be no room for those who complain that there is no point in working at your company.

Employees want to make a difference. This is, to be sure, "the very point of life." It is actually easy to help them do this when they are engaged and the business provides the right tools to get the work done. At the same time, the business must continually check employee engagement levels, asking employees how they feel about their work and whether they have the right tools to get the work done. It is also very important to give praise when warranted—and encouragement when things are not turning out quite as expected.

When working in a business that is designed to make a profit, Engaged Employees will clearly see "the very point of life." The profitability of their employer allows them to earn and function as good citizens in their community. Those who are not positive about the profit their employer earns are not the Right Fit; they should be released to work for a different employer in a different environment.

A key element here is to refrain from profit taking and stay constant with the idea of profit making. There is a difference, and it is an important one. Profit taking is typical in businesses where the employees are poorly compensated and not recognized for the quality of work that is being done. Business leaders who focus on profit taking literally step away from excellence in their operation. They forget that their people, the employees, are what make the difference.

WE ARE IN THE PEOPLE BUSINESS

I am often asked, "What business are you in?" I respond that we are in the people business. This notion has served us well, and it is inherently part of our Strategic Path. We are positioned to continue profitability in the right way because we know that business is all about the people and everything else—*everything*—is just details. We produce full value for others in order to earn our share of the profits. It works. It is a win-win situation for all the people with whom we come into contact.

Some people think that "the very point of life" has no place in a business. I understand their thinking; I just don't agree with it. Work matters to people, and we have designed a way to align our teams with meaningful and profitable work.

Ultimately, business building is nothing more than people building. Without engaged workers, no business will succeed. Thus, "the very point of life" could easily be defined as having the right people in the right role.

Well-being and kindness are qualities one can't turn on or off in a person. They are either real, or they are not. Rudeness is rooted out of our company, so we're left with fine, well-mannered people who are embraced for their goodness—for who they are, what they can give back, and how they can better express themselves in service to each other and customers. This is what it means to have the right people in the right role.

All this begs the question, What is the role of work in the life of people—employees, customers, and investors? While far beyond the scope of this book, it remains an essential question affecting every person. When a businessperson ignores this question and its impact in the workplace, it amounts to management malpractice. This isn't idealism or theory; it is life at its most fundamental and practical. When work brings expression to life, life is positive and productive . . . and the company is the residual beneficiary.

Few company leaders openly voice the fact that they don't value people, but people are often merely pawns in their game of business. Both actions and language, however, can reveal an elitist attitude of "us and them" (SMART Move 21). For these leaders, high employee turnover is an accepted cost of doing business, because "turning and burning" human resources is no different than any other purchased and sold company resource. Office supplies, electricity, and people are all seen as line items on the income statement, to be leased as cheaply as possible in order to make a profit.

Elitism, however, isn't limited to those people who sit at the boardroom table. In the context of the free enterprise system, it takes two participants to engage in this modern feudalistic embrace: the bosses and the workers. Each group is self-interested and distrustful of the other's motives. They've reached a tenuous peace held together only by individual advantage. The arrangement is all business, in the worst kind of way. Emotional pollution destructively seeps into every corner of the workplace. The business is divided, and everyone pays the price.

For decades, people have asked, "Does it have to be this way?" Our Strategic Path provides a meaningful and profitable alternative. I hope others, both within and outside of our company, discover a way to build upon the work we've begun. It isn't perfect, but it sure is producing great results.

CORE IDEOLOGY

Throughout the pages of this book, you've learned about some amazing people. According to Gallup, our team is one of the most engaged workforces in the world, across all industries and sectors. This fact constantly shocks people in both social and business settings. I keep getting asked, "How do you do that?"

This really is so simple, so basic: We value people—fellow team members, customers, and investors. That is our core ideology. Because we value people, we're in the business of building people up instead of tearing them down. Most of us want to make a difference with our lives, but putting that desire into practice can be confounding, especially in the workplace. Instead, many pursue the job that pays the most money over one that fulfills their personal purpose. This compromised approach of denying oneself for the love of money is a sellout, for all the wrong reasons.

We ask, why not pursue profit and purpose with vigor? It seems only logical that people who are working within their strengths in a Right Fit position and earning the rewards of prosperous pay for performance have the potential to ignite results. Our Strategic Path is revolutionary and in dramatic contrast to the highly compromised norms of doing business in corporate America, especially in the retail and service sectors. People will rise to the occasion of greatness when given the right chance, a bit of direction, and mutually beneficial incentives. As important as our Strategic Path is, however, it is still just an organizing map for those who lead and develop our people. This device of development must still be mastered in the hands of people who authentically value others and strive to advance their success.

When you first read about our Prosperous Wage Strategy, perhaps you were a skeptic. By now, I expect the logic of this strategy has become evident. In fact, as a responsible business, do we really have a choice? Our approach to compensation communicates up front that we value people differently than most companies do. We're paying the right people to join our team. This sends a clear and attractive message to prospective and existing team members. Next, we invest heavily and regularly in training our team members to succeed on the job, so they can reap even greater upside reward beyond their hourly wage. Service, respect, and reward are powerful allies in personal performance and satisfaction. Truly every role is important (SMART Move 20), because every person is valued.

Our Strategic Path allows us to walk our talk: We say that we value people, and we act accordingly. Monetary pay and excellent benefits are just the beginning of our compensation package. Having a manager committed to your success in life and work is another priceless element of that package. For people who are the Right Fit, we're extraordinarily accepting of quirks—provided that they're growing in their strengths and performance. This improved self-awareness and financial security frees our team members to more fully step into their "very point of life." Instead of heaping the debris of dissatisfied work on an employee's life, our push for performance actually scrapes off the layers of protective paint to get to the authentic person. Fewer on-the-job obstacles to success position our people for greater success in their jobs and as contributing members of society.

Collins and Porras's book *Built to Last* was a national business bestseller. Collins's next book, *Good to Great*, is equally esteemed in the business community. In chapter 9, titled "From Good to Great to Built to Last," Collins provides the essential link between the titles to his two bestselling business books. As a reader, when an author goes to this effort to connect his works, I stand up and take notice: There's something really special here. On page 215 is a section called: "Core Ideology: The Extra Dimension of Enduring Companies." Collins writes:

> That extra dimension is a guiding philosophy or a "core ideology" [that] consists of core values and core purpose (reason for being, beyond making money). These resemble the principles in the Declaration of Independence ("We hold these truths to be self-evident")—never perfectly followed, but always present as an inspiring standard and an answer to the question of *why* it is important that we exist.

In other words, core purpose and values are the common denominators of a business that is truly built to last and that can make the transition from good to great.

Our Strategic Path is our means of helping each person make the move from good to great *and* be built to last. It is a personal pathway to greatness for people first, before it is ever a powerful business system. It would remain inert, however, without our core ideology—our company culture—that we have discussed throughout the book and that will be described in greater detail in the final chapter. Our culture and our Strategic Path are always about the people.

I'm proud that our company provides a transformative experience for people, to create prosperity in both their pockets and their purpose. When I faced the monumental task of starting and building this company back in 1994, there was no Strategic Path. I had an inkling of a different and better way to do business, but I was guided more by instinct than by knowledge. My extensive reading habit furthered my understanding. I could not necessarily have articulated this ultimate intent, but in retrospect I see it clearly: The point of a business isn't profits for the sake of the money, but to become a serving corporation. Companies are simply a form of organizing people in such a way that they bind together with a core ideology to improve the universe of lives they touch along the SMART Moves Triangle—and perhaps even to create a ripple effect beyond that. To benefit the employees, the customers, and the investors, a robust and healthy profit-making motive is the essential high-octane fuel in the high-performance engine of transformation.

THE ORGANIZATIONAL FLAW CHART

With the advantage afforded by our Strategic Path, I now see other organizations differently. There's a design flaw crippling most businesses, and it has to do with the organizational chart—that simple, one-page document that shows the internal relationships of employees. The organizational chart has a role, mind you; it should be for defining functional lines of responsibility, period. Beyond that, it risks being a divisive and misdirecting document.

Ultimately, the point of the business is to serve the parties in the Triangle and the public good. Businesses, however, are typically organized by function. Look at an organizational chart. You'll see the president and CEO, with branches below for chiefs and vice presidents, including C-suite titles like chief operating officer, chief financial officer, and chief information officer plus positions like VP of marketing and VP of human resources. By design, each person has a functional responsibility, the expertise to back it up, and an accompanying point of view. There's a problem with this depiction of the business, however. The very structure of the organization creates silos of self-interested perspectives that work against the fundamental reasons for gathering all this talent in one place: to serve those within the Triangle. When function takes precedence over people, the business will inevitably fall short of its mark in terms of service and profit potential.

Most people gravitate to order, stability, and security. Therefore, if the organizational chart is the best depiction of how they're organized within the company, then these relationships are dominated by function. Focus instead on our Strategic Path, and you'll find that the functional teams are organized around what really matters: uniting all the people in the Triangle to score a win from each person's respective point of view. Each person has a defined role of contributing to a greater whole rather than simply providing a single, functional point of view. Living the Golden Rule (SMART Move 32) is actually the most rewarding result, provided that the "others" part is understood to be every participant around the Triangle. With this understanding in place, each person directs his or her talent on the core essence of the business rather than a narrow functional specialty. Integration and teamwork take precedence over expertise and functional turf.

Absent our Strategic Path or something like it, the only person charged with business integration is the president and CEO. In short, the CEO becomes the great coordinator and conductor of the business. That's a highly ineffective and inefficient model, yet it remains the traditional hierarchy in place today. Everyone gets so focused on looking up and down the organizational ladder for decisions and policies that they forget to look into the eyes of their teammates and customers . . . or even within themselves. "That's not my job" is the killer phrase indicating functional nearsightedness.

In the presence of our Strategic Path, each person has a profound understanding of how and why his or her work makes a contribution to the well-being of the other constituents along the Triangle. Individual effort is traceable to corporate performance in a "circle of life" kind of moment, where everything is connected to everything else. The thinking person gets it: "I've got a job to do. Others are depending upon me, and if I don't do my work with growing excellence then I'm fouling the system. I can't let down my friends—my peers and my customers. More important, I want to show them just how well I can perform within the customs of our culture."

Team members are selected and trained to make decisions on the spot and to be professional businesspersons. Our entire organization moves more fluidly and produces more abundantly. This redirection and integration of people's talent—coupled with training, tools, and resources—creates a productive alignment and cycling around the Triangle, resulting in Real Profit Increase that is reflected in a Stock Price Increase. The wealth of the nation is increased, and each person can see his or her individual contribution to the greater good.

Now that we've covered the length of our Strategic Path, let's put it into context. The final box in our figure—Stock Price Increase—is not so much an endpoint as an outcome reflective of how well we have executed and aligned the fundamentals all along the Strategic Path. This very defined and meticulously designed approach begins with a simple premise: We value people. This, to our company, is "the very point of life." It is an optimistic view of the inherent desire for an abundant life, the desire to reap rewards while being true to personal integrity. Through a growth process of competence and confidence, people live to their full potential and reap the rewards of their success by doing the right thing and by doing things right.

Where we are today, as a company and as the people inextricably linked to that company, is because of our Strategic Path. I can't imagine what state we would be in if we didn't have it. Our team is the most competent, kind, and productive the world has ever seen. As a result, we are the world's most profitable in our industry on a per store basis. First, value people; then the people will return the kindness and the profits! This, then, is "the very point of life."

CHAPTER SUMMARY

KEY POINTS

- Ultimately, business building is people building. As easy as it is to get caught up in the disciplines of business—marketing, finance, operations, HR, and so forth—people are the defining advantage.

- Work is an important part of life, but it is not "the very point of life." The value one places on people is the vital defining question: Are they cogs in the gears of industry or cocreators in the development of a good or service?

- Core ideology informs the design, development, and operation of the business. Our Strategic Path is indicative of our high esteem of the inherent value of people. It provides us with a clear path to ensure that we have on board the most qualified people committed to our common cause.

CHAPTER 14

FINAL WORDS:
HOW DOES BEING "ALL ABOUT PEOPLE" LEAD TO CONSISTENT PERFORMANCE AND PROFITABILITY?

A company must have a core ideology to become a visionary company. It must also have an unrelenting drive for progress. And finally, it must be well designed as an organization to preserve the core and stimulate progress with all the key pieces working in alignment. These are the universal requirements for visionary companies.

James Collins and Jerry Porras, *Built to Last*

IN CHAPTER 1, WE DEALT WITH THE QUESTION, HOW DO YOU DO THAT? Customers always want to know how we achieve world-class results while consistently satisfying your employees, customers, and investors alike. The answer, in a phrase, is this: We hire our people with science and hold them together with leadership and culture. Our Strategic Path is our science, and in this final chapter, we'll turn our full attention to our company culture.

Collins and Porras open their book by providing the "universal requirements" for a company to be built to last. Borrowing their terms, our Strategic Path is our means to preserve our core, stimulate progress, and align all the key pieces of the business. It addresses three of their four requirements for being a visionary company. The fourth requirement is core ideology; we refer to that as our culture. Let me give you a glimpse into our core strategic intent: not just how we do business but, more important, *why* we do business and what guides our decisions.

Our Strategic Path and our company culture together explain completely the SMART Moves Triangle discussed in chapter 1 and clearly describe what powers our consistent performance at unprecedented levels of profitability. One without the other is inefficient and ineffective. Here's an analogy: If our Strategic Path is a series of electrical junction boxes connected by cables, then our culture is the main power source— the electricity running through the large cord. The degree to which they each maintain their integrity and are in sync with one another determines the potential output of our company.

Power needs a conduit to express its intended purpose. Culture is power, and our Strategic Path is the cord. Individually, each has a dormant capacity; together, they can light up our people, our company, our industry, the world. Our culture, therefore, must be not only powerful but also stable. Our Strategic Path must offer integrity of design and high standards of construction. Should either falter, the entire system will short and will fail to fulfill its capacity.

Culture matters! Every company has a culture and a business model, regardless of its level of awareness. An ad hoc or jerry-rigged model impedes progress and creates waste. Likewise, a low-wattage culture can't light up a company with results. A wavering culture produces dirty power filled with unpredictable spikes and surges. Failure to articulate core ideology risks brownouts or blown fuses all along our Strategic Path. Any of these conditions disrupts results.

Our culture relies on the high standards and sound construction of our Strategic Path. A flawed or fragile cable limits throughput. When lofty intentions meet low bandwidth and breakdowns, then effectiveness and efficiencies are diminished by frustration. Business growth is stunted, and profits are constrained. On the other hand, people can thrive in a dependable, highly defined, strong corporate culture that is regularly communicated, reinforced, and monitored. Good things happen when the business model and culture are concisely integrated.

Our Strategic Path is *how we do what we do*. It is structured and engineered by a unique purpose, toward a vision, through a narrow mission, and with values to guide it. The logical and linear nature of our Strategic Path is particularly comforting to left-brained thinkers. Knowing the rules of the game is the only way to play fair. This orderly progression from one step to the other is challenging to build, yet when planned with care, it is predictable and doable. Most of all, it is essential to fully realize the service capacity and profit potential inherent in the business opportunity.

Culture, on the other hand, is about *who we are*. It involves the raw power of people to imagine, dream, innovate, and achieve. There is no power on the planet greater than the human spirit engaged in meaningful work. An identity and direction harnesses who we are and what we do so we can serve a greater good.

Culture is mystical and fluid, capable of being grasped yet not held still. It remains largely unexplored and untapped by most leaders because of the mysterious nature of humankind. Culture is corporate and yet profoundly personal. To press into culture is to press into the life of another person. Generally, this is a risky, awkward, and unnatural place for leaders. It gets written off as "too soft" and "touchy-feely." Nothing could be further from the truth. To whom does leadership apply? People! People are the very essence of organizational leadership.

Leadership is supported, however, by process and procedures. Our culture and our Strategic Path may well be the greatest leadership and management development program in the world, simply because these tried-and-true elements prepare a manager and team for openness, honesty, and trust, all within our system of high performance standards.

PERFORMANCE THAT NEVER PEAKS

To say we're all about the people—employees, customers, investors— sounds noble, but we must dignify our intention with action. Our Strategic Path is the structural part of making it happen; our company culture is the people side. As strong as we are, we're still on the frontier of tapping the latent power of our people. A store never peaks in earnings when a team has inspiration, innovation, and personal incentives. Culture is the next great source of advancement for any profit-making enterprise, especially ours.

Core ideology informs our company culture just as the principles of the Constitution inform American culture. We're pioneers in our company and our industry, not cartographers for every business—though we have a road map that's worth following. We can chart a productive and profitable course, thanks to our Strategic Path. Yet it is a constant learning process, not a set of guidelines written in stone. Culture is dynamic and alive because it is about the people.

Getting acquainted with our people begins casually and develops over time into a more personal conversation. First they learn about our Strategic Path—*what we do* in our business. Along the way, as we spend some time together, we take the conversation to that deeper place: our company culture, or *who we are* in fundamental terms. We introduce you to our culture through this natural approach of "getting to know someone," starting with our mission, continuing through our vision and the values that guide it, and ending with our purpose. What follows is an abbreviated version of our strategic statements—from the work we do, to how we see things, and finally moving to the guts and heart of our business.

Mission Statement (what we do): *Focus on winning!*

- Being the most profitable pawn chain in the world in terms of return on investment
- Having an open culture of trust and accountability among our team members
- Delivering the best customer service through 100 percent application of standards
- Having the highest paid and wealthiest team members in the industry

Our Vision (what we see): *We are the best in the world.*
- Excellence in Every Role—People
- Green and Clean—Place
- Beat Budgets

Our Values (what is important to our decisions).
- Learning
- Execution
- Cleanliness
- Celebration
- Kindness

Our Purpose (why we do what we do): *Cultivating greatness.*

Our Place in the World (the grand perspective): *The pursuit of happiness.*

Our final and overall mantra is to move toward education—not just for the sake of learning, but to ensure action that will allow everyone to win and help the company to make a profit. Remember, if an issue is not actionable, then you probably should not waste your time talking about it. Your people and your actions will tell the tale. Profits are yours for the asking.

BIBLIOGRAPHY

Buckingham, Marcus, and Donald O. Clifton. *Now, Discover Your Strengths.* New York: The Free Press, 2001.

Buckingham, Marcus, and Curt Coffman. *First, Break All The Rules: What the World's Greatest Managers Do Differently.* New York: Simon & Schuster, 1999.

Chernow, Ron. *Titan: The Life of John D. Rockefeller, Sr.* New York: Random House Inc., 1998.

Coffman, Curt, and Gabriel Gonzalez-Molina. *Follow This Path: How the World's Greatest Organizations Drive Growth by Unleashing Human Potential.* New York: Warner Books, 2002.

Collins, James C. and Jerry I. Porras. *Built to Last.* New York: HarperCollins Publishers, 1994.

Collins, Jim. *Good to Great.* New York: HarperCollins Publishers, 2001.

Covey, Stephen R. *The 7 Habits of Highly Effective People.* New York: Simon & Schuster, 1990.

Drucker, Peter F. *The Effective Executive: The Definitive Guide to Getting the Right Things Done.* New York: HarperCollins Publishers, 2006.

Ford, Henry. *Moving Forward.* Reprinted. New York: Kessinger Publishing, 2003.

Ford, Henry. *My Life and Work.* Reprinted. New York: Kessinger Publishing, 2003.

Ford, Henry. *Today and Tomorrow.* Reprinted. New York: Productivity Press, 2003.

Holtz, Lou. *Wins, Losses, and Lessons.* New York: William Morrow, 2006.

Mansfield, Harvey C., trans. *The Prince: Niccolò Machiavelli.* 2nd ed. Chicago: University of Chicago Press, 1998.

Ogilvy, David. *Confessions of an Advertising Man.* 2nd ed. New York: Simon & Schuster, 1988.

Phillips, Donald T. *Lincoln on Leadership: Executive Strategies for Tough Times.* New York: Warner Books, 1992.

Rath, Tom, and Donald O. Clifton. *How Full Is Your Bucket?: Positive Strategies for Work and Life.* New York: Gallup Press, 2004.

Reichheld, Frederick F., and Thomas Teal. *The Loyalty Effect: The Hidden Force Behind Growth, Profits, and Lasting Value.* Boston: Harvard Business School Press, 2001.

Smart, Bradford D. *Topgrading: How Leading Companies Win by Hiring, Coaching, and Keeping the Best People.* Rev. ed. New York: Portfolio, 2005.

Smith, Benson, and Tony Rutigliano. *Discover Your Sales Strengths: How the World's Greatest Salespeople Develop Winning Careers.* New York: Warner Books, 2003.

Wagner, Rodd, and James K. Harter, PhD. *12: The Elements of Great Managing.* New York: Gallup Press, 2006.

Watson, Jr., Thomas J. *A Business and Its Beliefs: The Ideas That Helped Build IBM.* New York: McGraw-Hill Book Company, Inc., 1963.

Welch, Jack, with Suzy Welch. *Winning.* New York: HarperCollins Publishers, 2005.

ABOUT THE AUTHOR

John Thedford knows what it takes to succeed in this world. He'll quickly tell you that "it's not about *I.Q.* it's about *I Do*." And he has been a doer for as long as he can remember. His tireless efforts have made him successful as he has built world-class companies and been recognized for his achievements. However, he believes his best work is ahead of him.

When John launched Value Financial, a chain of successful pawn shops, his shops defied the stereotype of the typical pawn shop. Clean, profitable, loaded with talented and long-tenured managers and associates, these were true financial centers for the communities they served.

John is a great judge of talent and understands the power of having the right person in the right role. A few years after establishing Value Financial, John met a successful executive in a furniture rental business and decided to raise the capital to give him the opportunity to run his own furniture rental operation. This organization, *Rent-Rite*, was cited as #4 in Inc. Magazine's annual list of the 500 fastest-growing companies in America in 2003. Rent-Rite would eventually sell to Rent-a-Center.

A few years after the sale of *Rent-Rite* and well into over a decade of uninterrupted success, John sold Value Financial Services. What's next included writing *Smart Moves Management,* a how-to book that explains in detail how any leader can use the latest and most reliable techniques to build great sales and management teams. The book explains clearly how Thedford took theoretical management ideas and wove them into his organization in a practical way to produce first class results.